Two Men

Articles on Practical Christian Living

Bill Hall

DEWARD
PUBLISHING COMPANY

Foreword

Practical. Jesus does not want the truth to be taught just theoretically; He also wants it to be applied. That's how He taught. His sermons stir us because they bring His profound insights right down to where we live. When He showed the shortcomings of the traditional Jewish interpretations of the law (Matt 5), He spoke not just about anger, but of how it is displayed; not just about adultery, but of what we look at; not just about love, but of exactly what to do when we meet an enemy. As He warned of self-righteousness (Matt 6), He discussed giving alms, praying and fasting, and specified guidelines in each area.

It is much easier to expound a doctrine than to apply it. Applications tend to be trite, strained, or vague. It's especially tough to apply deeper principles—like humility, godliness, or worship. While these articles by Bill Hall are certainly well-studied and insightful, most of all they are practical. They step on our toes. They clarify the application of spiritual principles in life and encourage us to be stronger Christians.

For years before I knew Bill Hall I admired his writing—especially his articles contrasting two men/preachers/churches, etc. I often wished I had a book of his articles that I could give to friends.

When I moved to Alabama in the early 90s, I was blessed with the opportunity to get acquainted with Bill and Charlotte. I saw that the articles which had encouraged me so much in my daily Christian life had been written by a brother who was serious about living it himself, a brother who demonstrates the seasoned character and dedication of one who has effectively preached the gospel for several decades. Our friendship has helped me.

I appreciate Bill permitting me to publish his articles. I hope and pray that they help you as much as they have helped me.

Gary Fisher

Contents

Chapter Nine: Encouragement

Chapter Ten: Church

Chapter Eleven: Teaching/Leading

Chapter Twelve: Tough Questions

Chapter Thirteen: Family

Chapter Fourteen: Brief Points

Two Men Can't Agree on Religion

Two men are religious, and both seem to be sincere, but they never seem to agree on religious questions. A brief look at their applications of the Bible helps to explain their problem.

The first man views the Bible as the complete and final answer to all religious questions pertaining to salvation. For him a clear statement from the Bible ends all controversy. His simple approach is well stated by a bumper sticker we have seen: "God said it; I believe it; that settles it." In fact, he would agree that God's word "settles it" whether he believes it or not.

The second man relies on several sources for his religious beliefs. He believes the Bible and many of his convictions are based on what the Bible says. But he also is convinced that he has been "led" into certain beliefs by the Lord. Some of those beliefs he could not defend by the Bible, and in fact some of them seem to contradict the Bible, but he is sure that they are true, for the Lord would not have so "led" him had they not been true. One man frankly said to this writer, "I read the Bible, but I mostly just depend on the Spirit to lead me in what I believe." He has also had his beliefs verified by knowledgeable preachers, who might not be right in everything, but would hardly be wrong on any serious question of truth.

The first man reads the Bible seeking for answers from God. **The second man** reads the Bible for the same reason, but his perception is affected by what he has been "led to believe." He has difficulty being objective, and, in fact, he might hold to what he has been "led to believe" ahead of plain teaching of scripture. He frankly finds his likeness in the man of Colossians 2.18-19 who takes "his stand on visions he has seen" and is "not holding fast to the Head" (NASB). His religious practices may be different from the man described in Colossians, but his approach to authority in religion is the same.

2 | Two Men

We do not hesitate to side with the first man in his approach. God indeed "leads" us into truth, but He does so through His inspired word. Consider the following passages: "Your word is a lamp to my feet and a light to my path" (Psa 119.105). "Sanctify them by Your truth. Your word is truth" (John 17.17). "All Scripture is given by inspiration of God, and is profitable for doctrine, for reproof, for correction, for instruction in righteousness, that the man of God may be complete, thoroughly equipped for every good work" (2 Tim 3.16-17).

The two men of our article will come to remarkable agreement when they both approach the scriptures as the final word from God, but not until then. Religious differences are not the product of scripture, but of varying attitudes toward what constitutes final authority in religion. True unity is desirable, and it can be enjoyed by those who humbly submit to God's word and will.

Two Men 'Know' They Are Saved

Two men "know" they are saved.

The first man bases his assurance of salvation on his experience. He had been assured that when he completely turned his life over to Jesus Christ, accepted Him as his personal Savior, and received Him into his heart, that an inner peace and feeling of well-being would sweep his soul; that he would be able to recognize that feeling when it came; and that his peace and feeling of well-being would be unmistakable evidence of his salvation. In keeping with that teaching he did "receive Jesus into his heart." He did feel this wonderful peace sweep his soul. And he "knows" that he is saved.

The second man's assurance is based on the promise of God. He had read in God's word, "He who believes and is baptized will be saved" (Mark 16.16). From other passages he had learned the necessity of repentance and confession of faith (Acts 2.38; 8.37; Rom 10.10). Trusting God's promise of salvation, he obeyed from the heart those commands (Rom 6.17), and has never doubted since that God forgave him of all his past sins, according to His promise.

The first man's assurance of salvation is based upon an unsure foundation. The Bible teaches neither the action he has taken nor the criterion he has accepted. We do not question his feelings; but we do question that such feelings are proof of salvation, for they are the product of his teaching. The cultist who has been taught certain gross practices in religion and has become the victim of his perverted leader will experience similar feelings. If the feelings of the latter are not sufficient proof of salvation, neither are the feelings of the former.

"But an angel appeared and spoke to me," someone may be thinking; or, "I spoke in tongues." The Bible teaches, however, that even unusual, inexplicable occurrences in one's life cannot set aside the teaching of God's revealed word. Many who will be in Hell will have said, "Lord, Lord, have we not prophesied in Your name, cast out demons in Your name, and done many wonders in Your name?" (Matt 7.22). But all their experiences, even "miracles," will not substitute for their doing the Father's will as it is recorded in the scriptures (Matt 7.21; see also Gal 1.8; 2 Thes 2.9-12; Deut 13.1-5; Col 2.18-19).

The second man has based his assurance on a solid foundation. God's promises are sure. He cannot lie (Heb 6.18). What He has promised He is able to perform (Rom 4.21). The person who obeys His commandments through trust in His promises can know, because God is faithful. "Now by this we know that we know Him, if we keep His commandments" (1 John 2.3).

We ask our readers, "Who really demonstrates strong faith in God: the one who simply trusts God's promises and finds assurance in His word or the one who must experience some overwhelming feeling that sweeps his soul?" God's judgment will be based, not on what we "know," but on His word. Be not deceived!

Two Men Err Regarding Grace

Two men err regarding grace. **The first man** preaches grace, but fails to recognize that God's grace is linked to human responsibility. **The second man** preaches responsibility, but seldom speaks of God's grace.

The first man believes that salvation is solely by God's grace. He contends that any required action on man's part in obedience to commands would nullify grace and would constitute meritorious salvation. "It is absurd to believe that God's grace could be linked to anything like baptism," is the way one person stated it.

The second man speaks well of the requirements of the gospel. He often preaches the necessity of baptism, faithful attendance, liberal giving, good morals, doing one's part in the activities of the local church, etc. He speaks of Jesus as our perfect example and of His full submission to the Father in His death, but rarely of Him as the propitiation for our sins. Seldom does he bring his listeners to feel their constant need for God's mercy and forgiveness and their absolute helplessness and hopelessness apart from the cleansing blood of Christ.

The first man would promise salvation without the necessary diligence in learning and doing God's will. **The second man** would place so much emphasis on learning and doing God's will that he would focus the eyes of his listeners more on themselves than upon the Lord. **The first man** needs to learn the truth of Titus 2.11-12: "For the grace of God that brings salvation has appeared to all men, teaching us that, denying ungodliness and worldly lusts, we should live soberly, righteously, and godly in the present age." **The second man** needs to learn and appreciate the exhortation of Philippians 3.1: "Finally, my brethren, rejoice in the Lord."

We would remind **the first man** of the nature of God's grace as it is revealed throughout the ages. We would begin with God's grace as it was extended to Noah at the time of the flood. "Noah found grace in the eyes of the LORD" (Gen 6.8). Noah, however, was given instructions to be obeyed. And Noah recognized the necessity of obedience: "Thus Noah did; according to all that God commanded him, so he did" (Gen 6.22). Had Noah failed in his responsibilities, he would never have been saved from the flood by the grace of God. We would remind this man of God's grace as it was extended to Joshua in the capture of Jericho. "See! I have given Jericho into your hand" (Josh 6.2). But God had instructions for Joshua: march, blow the trumpets, shout. When Joshua and the Israelites fulfilled their responsibilities "the wall fell down flat. Then the people went up into the city" (Josh 6.20). We would remind this man of the blind man of John 9 whose eyes the Lord opened (John 9.14,17,21,26,30) when he did what the Lord commanded. Our first man should be able to see that: (1) God's grace does not rule out instructions (law); (2) God's grace does not rule out obedience; and (3) God's grace does not rule out strict obedience.

We would remind **the second man** that good works without God's grace can never save. We would begin with the message of Ephesians. Paul in Ephesians did indeed give instructions—practical instructions, instructions that must be obeyed, concerning morals, duties of wives, husbands, children, parents, servants, masters—but not until he had firmly established God's grace as the basis of salvation (chs 1-3) and as the motivation for obedience to God's instructions (observe the word "therefore" in 4.1). We would remind this man of the danger of being like the Pharisees who "trusted in themselves that they were righteous, and despised others" (Luke 18.9-14). We would remind him that when one sins he has "nothing to pay" and therefore must approach God as one who is poor in spirit, mourning, meek, and hungering and thirsting after righteousness (Luke 7.41-42; Matt 5.3-6).

We would not dare to say which of these teachers is the more dangerous, for they both err regarding grace. We find ourselves naturally recoiling at the teaching of the first man and greatly fearing the consequences of his teaching, but we never want to be guilty of the error of the second. We cannot preach grace without preaching responsibility, but we must not be guilty of preaching responsibility without preaching grace.

Two Men Seek Faith

Two men seek faith. **The first man's** approach is to try to find solutions to all the problems. He has delved deeply into the difficult questions relating to the Genesis account of creation. He has read volumes on the flood. He finds the story of Jonah particularly challenging. He relies heavily on archaeology and secular history for confirmation of his solutions. He believes **because** he is satisfied with his own answers to the problems of faith.

The second man's approach centers upon Jesus Christ. He too has had to consider evidences and struggle with certain problems, but he is fully persuaded that Jesus Christ is the Son of God and has confessed that he believes that fact with all his heart. Believing in Jesus as the infallible Son of God, he does not question anything Jesus believed, anything Jesus said, or anything Jesus authorized to be said.

He, too, wondered about the Genesis account of creation, but his questions ceased when he read the words of Jesus: "Have you not read that He who made them at the beginning 'made them male and female,' and said, 'For this reason a man shall leave his father and mother and be joined to his wife, and the two shall become one flesh?'" (Matt 19.4-5). If Jesus' stamp of approval was on the creation story, that was good enough for him. He didn't have the solution to all the problems, but he believed **because** Jesus believed it, and he believed in Jesus.

His faith in other Old Testament accounts was similarly established. He found Jesus' stamp of approval on the flood (Matt 24.37-39) and the story of Jonah (Matt 12.40), and in fact, on all the Old Testament record in one sweeping statement recorded in Luke 24.44: "Then He said to them, 'These are the words which I spoke to you while I was still with you, that all things must be fulfilled which were written in the Law of Moses and the Prophets and the Psalms concerning Me.'"

Since the New Testament contains what Jesus said combined with what He authorized to be said, the second man had no trouble believing the New Testament. His faith in the whole Bible simply rests upon his faith in Christ as the infallible Son of God. He too finds the study of the problems of faith intriguing and challenging, but his own personal faith is not dependent on finding solutions to all the problems.

The first man's faith stands on shaky ground, for it is founded on human wisdom. Should some later archaeological discovery or other bit of evidence not now known prove his solutions to be false, the very foundation of his faith would be gone. He would have to seek new solutions or lose his faith entirely.

The second man's faith may not appeal to the highly sophisticated, but it is founded on the rock—on the One who is "the same yesterday, today, and forever" (Heb 13.8).

"So then faith comes by hearing, and hearing by the word of God" (Rom 10.17).

Two Men Serve the Lord

Two men serve the Lord. **The first** is motivated by his love for the local church as an institution. He enthusiastically supports its program of activities. He works diligently to get others to be baptized, for he is interested in this organization of which he is a part, and he wants to see it grow. He attends all the meetings, gives liberally of his money, and really does his part in support of the local church.

The other is motivated by his love for the Lord. He, too, works to convert others, but he does so because he is concerned for their souls. He, too, attends all the meetings, for in doing so he is drawn closer to the Lord whom he loves, and has opportunity to glorify His name. He also gives liberally of his money, for he loves the Lord and is interested in doing his part in financing His work. He loves the church and rejoices when it grows but his love reaches far more deeply than does that of the first man; in fact, he would serve the Lord if there were not another Christian on earth nor prospects that there would ever be another.

The first man's enthusiasm is dependent to a great degree on others. While the congregation is growing and active, his enthusiasm continues strong; but when problems arise, or his favorite preacher moves on, or some of his brethren don't "pull their weight," or someone criticizes him, or the congregation just generally faces a difficult period, his enthusiasm begins to wane, and he becomes "unfaithful."

The second man is stable and unwavering. Brethren come and go; the congregation of which he is a part has its periods of depression; problems arise from time to time; but this man's enthusiasm remains constant through it all, for it is centered on Him who never changes, the One who has promised, "I will never leave you nor forsake you."

Let us take heed, then, how we build (1 Cor 3.10). Perhaps the title of this article should read, "One Man Serves the Lord," for it is very doubtful that the first man serves the Lord at all.

Two Men View Strictness

Two men determine to obey the scriptures strictly. Neither wants to turn "to the right hand or to the left," even in the least matter. But the attitudes behind the determination of these two men vary tremendously.

The first man views strictness in obeying God's law as the primary means of salvation. While he speaks academically of the grace of God, practically he gives little thought to his continual need for God's grace. He determines to attend every service, give liberally, live by a rigorous code of conduct in his daily life, maintain control of his family; in short, he is really "going to live his religion." While preaching that a man cannot be saved by meritorious works, he unconsciously sets out to do the very thing that he preaches one cannot do.

The second man recognizes God's grace as the primary means of salvation. He speaks frequently of divine mercy that could extend even to himself. He is just as strict in obeying God's word as the first man. He, too, attends every service, gives liberally, etc., but his careful obedience to every command is a manifestation of his love for God (John 14.15), his faith in God's promises (Jas 2.20), and his realization that God's grace is extended only to those who do obey Him (Matt 7.21). Knowing how far short of God's perfection he will fall, however, he determines to turn constantly to God for forgiveness and mercy. His only boast will be that of the cross.

One of two things will happen to **the first man**. Either he will convince himself that he really is "living his religion"—that he really is succeeding in living up to that standard which he has set for himself—in which case he will, in his self-righteousness, despise the struggling weak ones who can't live up to his supposed level of righteousness ("Also He spoke this parable to some who trusted in themselves that they were righteous, and despised others" Luke 18.9); or, he will grow discouraged as he honestly recognizes his failures, and throw up his hands in despair. "I tried," he will say, "but I just couldn't live it." Either way, the man is doomed, for his thinking is wrong.

The second man will find real joy in the Lord and peace which passeth all understanding. He will live in constant hope, a hope built not on his own perfection, but on the assurance of God's forgiveness. He will be longsuffering to the weak and immature, for he will be well aware of his own unworthiness before God. He will not seek to put on some hypocritical front, for he will never claim to be anything but a sinner saved by grace.

Our two men will appear to be very similar on the outside in their strictness toward the scriptures (both will probably be called "legalists"), but there will be a marked difference on the inside, and we are quite sure that there will be considerable difference in the ultimate direction and outcome of their lives.

Two Men React to Teaching on Morals

Two men listen to lessons on practical Christian living, but their attitudes differ greatly.

The first man views all such teaching as arbitrary "church" rules. Warnings concerning dancing, mixed swimming, general immodesty, divorce for every cause, drinking, etc., are all looked upon as "Church of Christ" standards, traditions being sustained by the old-timers of the church who are out of touch with more up-to-date thinking on morals.

The second man is brought to understand that all such teaching is an outgrowth of genuine respect for the Bible; that warnings concerning the evils mentioned above are based on such scriptures as Matthew 5.27-28; Galatians 5.19-21; 1 Timothy 2.9; Matthew 19.9; and Romans 13.12-14; that they, therefore, are not arbitrary church rules, but are indeed a true picture of God's will for His people.

The first man hates this teaching. Of course he does! Doesn't he have just as much moral perception as another? Why should he allow some other man to decide what's right or what's wrong for him? He'll do what he pleases. Nobody will bind his thinking on him.

The second man, recognizing that the standards under consideration are God's and not men's, gladly complies. Jesus Christ is his

Lord and King. He will live whatever life his Lord wants him to live. He will make every sacrifice his Lord wants him to make. His conformity grows out of a desire to please God, not man.

The first man may take the form of a teenager rebelling against parental authority; or the form of a man "raised in the church," whose church loyalty is beginning to wane; or the form of a new convert who is having difficulty defining modesty, decency, and lasciviousness in practical terms. The fault may lie within the person himself. He may want to break away from all restrictions, thus refusing to view objectively Bible principles behind the teaching he is rejecting. Or the fault in some cases may lie in those who teach. They may be guilty of "establishing" their points along these lines through pulpit beating and foot stamping, rather than through sound reasoning from the scriptures; of unconsciously seeking for "church" loyalty or "preacher" loyalty rather than loyalty to the Lord. Either way, we are concerned for our first man's soul, for he is wrong in his thinking.

Let no one misunderstand. We strongly oppose every evil mentioned above. But the truth is—no man is obligated to bow to anything **we** teach because **we** teach it; but, on the other hand, he is obligated to live by every principle that is truly established upon the word of God. It is the duty of every teacher, then, to warn of these evils, but on the basis of God's authority. It is the duty of every hearer to consider them in the light of scripture. Greater God-consciousness—on the part of both teacher and hearer—is the need.

Three Men Rebel Against Hypocrisy

Three men rebel against hypocrisy, but they vary greatly in their reactions. **The first man** turns to total moral abandonment. He throws off all restraint as he gives himself to the fulfillment of every fleshly desire. "Self" becomes his god. He hardens himself to the tears of his family as he goes out to do what he wants to do. His "justification" for his shameful conduct: "At least I'm not a hypocrite!"

The second man goes to an opposite extreme. He is fed up with the weakness and hypocrisy that he sees in all the churches, and he is not going to be like such people. He will become a Christian and from the beginning "he's going to live it." He will be an example of what a Christian really ought to be. To him, the cure for hypocrisy is perfection.

The third man wants to avoid hypocrisy in his life, but at the same time, he has a deep sense of his own imperfection. So he takes on no air of infallibility, but sets out to be genuine. His genuineness soon becomes apparent to others. He does not claim perfection, but he strives for perfection. As he worships God, he does not claim to be perfect as a worshiper, but when the singing begins he gives his heart to what he's doing; when the prayer is led, he listens and makes the prayer his prayer; during the supper he meditates on the suffering of his Lord; and throughout the sermon he participates in a study of God's word; if his mind wanders, he brings it back; and when the worship period ends he asks God to forgive him for his failure and to accept his worship in spite of his imperfection.

When he goes to his job, he does not claim perfection among his fellow workers, but they know that he will try to give eight hours of work for eight hours of pay; that he is trustworthy; that he is pure in his speech and life; and that if he is ever overcome by pressures around him to sin, he will humbly seek the forgiveness of those who have been wronged.

He is the same in his home. His family respects him because he is genuine and does not claim strength and goodness beyond reality. His family sees his faults, but his one redeeming quality that enables him to maintain their respect is his ability to say, "I'm sorry." In every area of his life, he walks humbly before his God and his fellowman.

Our third man has found the true cure for hypocrisy. **The first man,** if he does not repent, will someday be a miserable wretch, his life completely torn and shattered. **The second man** is headed for disillusionment. His goals are unreal; his outlook is totally wrong. But the man who "walks humbly with his God" and is wholly free from guile is a blessed man indeed. He is in life and attitude what God wants him to be, and he lives in hope of heaven.

"Blessed are the poor in spirit, for theirs is the kingdom of heaven" (Matt 5.3).

Two Men Attend Worship Services

Two men attend worship services. **The first man** attends wholly out of a sense of duty. He understands the teaching of Hebrews 10.25: "Not forsaking the assembling of ourselves together," and is determined to obey faithfully that teaching. He will not allow anything within his power to stand in the way of his attending the worship periods of the church.

The second man recognizes his duty in this matter, too, but his primary motivation in attendance is his love for the Lord and his joy in blending his voice and heart with other Christians in praise and adoration to the Lord. He delights in worship and the spiritual strength he derives through worship.

The first man is mentally passive throughout the worship service. If the words of the song happen to catch his attention, he observes and appreciates them; otherwise, he just sings along with little concern for what he is singing. If the sermon is interesting, he listens; otherwise, he just relaxes, and hopes the time won't drag too badly. He does meditate briefly concerning Christ's suffering and death as he partakes of the supper, for somehow the importance of the memorial feast has been impressed upon his mind.

The second man comes mentally prepared to worship. He pays close attention to the words of each song and makes the sentiment of the songs his own sentiment. In fact, he sometimes studies the words of frequently used songs so he will be sure he understands their meaning. Depth of meaning is of greater importance to him than a catchy tune or rhythmic beat. He listens to each phrase of the prayer that is led, and if he can approve the petitions of the prayer, he unites with the one who leads with his "Amen." He discerns the Lord's body as he breaks bread, and he listens carefully to the sermon, volunteering his attention, hiding the word in his heart, that he might not sin against God (Psa 119.11). If his mind wanders occasionally, he brings it back to the worship. He worships with a consciousness of God as the object of his worship, the One toward whom these expressions of adoration are directed.

The first man reduces his service to a mere code of external rites, while **the second man** obeys "from the heart," combining the outward with the inward. **The first man** is more likely to be satisfied with his service to the Lord, for he has accepted the easier standard, but it is **the second man** who enjoys God's approval. "God is Spirit, and those who worship Him must worship in spirit and truth" (John 4.24).

We ask the reader: "In which of these two men do you see a reflection of yourself?" The need is obvious! We must cast off our laziness and indifference, revitalize our spirits, and bring ourselves to worship God acceptably. There is a considerable difference between mere attendance of a worship service and truly acceptable worship.

Two Men Try to Worship

Worship under the best of conditions can sometimes be difficult. Distractions, human error, and sometimes funny situations can occur to take one's attention away from the Lord. Attitudes, however, can prove to be a major factor in acceptable (or non-acceptable) worship. For instance…

Two men sincerely try to worship. **The first man**, though, is frustrated throughout. His frustrations begin with the opening announcements when the man in charge takes ten minutes to say what any normal man could say in three. He is hardly over that when the song leader adds to his frustrations, selecting a song he is sure contains an unscriptural phrase. The man who presides at the table doesn't help when he uses the term "loaf" instead of "bread" and then the man who is called on to "give thanks for the bread" gives thanks for everything but the bread. The preacher makes a major contribution by totally misapplying a passage of scripture ("He probably didn't spend enough time on that one," the man thinks). When the worship period is finally dismissed, he tries to share his frustrations with those around him, but no one seems to care.

The second man observes many of the mistakes the first man observes. In fact, without fanfare he just doesn't sing the questionable phrase in the song and he silently thanks God for the bread when he realizes the leader's failure to do so. But while observing mistakes, he focuses attention on the good sentiments of the songs that are used and on the death of his Savior during the Lord's Supper. He makes the prayer that is led his own and appreciates the good thoughts presented in the lesson. He has come to worship God. He makes allowances for human frailty on the part of the leaders in worship, appreciates their sincere efforts, and refuses to let their mistakes keep him from his purpose.

The first man is to be pitied. His ability to "worship" is dependent on the ability of the leaders in the worship period, and any half-observant person knows how inept that leadership can be at times. He comes to worship, but spends the hour criticizing. He blames others for that which is really his own problem. Consequently, his problem with worship becomes a problem also with his brethren; but one cannot have a problem with his worship and his brethren without having a problem in his relationship with God.

The second man, by maintaining a positive attitude toward his brethren, even when they make mistakes, is able to worship acceptably and is drawn closer to God by his worship.

We are not condoning sloppily conducted worship periods. Leaders in worship should seek to avoid mistakes and to do their work effectively. But acceptable worship depends far more on the heart and attitude of the worshiper than on the abilities of leaders. Our first man may point the finger of blame at others, but his real need is a total change of attitude within himself.

Two Men Face Their Limitations

Two men are rather inept in areas of public leadership. Neither is really talented in leading singing, preaching, teaching Bible classes, or fulfilling other roles that are so essential to effective worship periods. Both have tried, but their inabilities in such realms are apparent, to themselves and to others. But while they share this limitation, their attitudes differ dramatically.

The first man draws back into a shell, manifesting all the symptoms of an inferiority complex. He feels that he doesn't belong, that others don't appreciate him. He does nothing for the benefit of the Lord's cause except to attend. He rarely visits the sick or speaks to a visitor or invites a newcomer into his home. "Can't" becomes the prevailing word in his vocabulary. He complains because "only a few are running things."

The second man, recognizing his obvious inabilities in leadership roles, looks about for other areas in which he can be helpful. He volunteers to keep the grass mowed around the building and to see that the building is opened early at every service. He is there to extend a warm greeting to the first arrivals. This is just typical of him. He is constantly observing a need and is working in his own quiet way to take care of that need.

No other man in the church is more active in the work than he is.

The first man struggles to be faithful. His feelings are so easily hurt. Every lesson that deals with greater diligence in the Lord's service is preached directly with him in mind, he is sure. He doesn't like himself and his attitude is a barrier to good relationships with others.

The second man is appreciated by all who know him. His influence is great. He is perfectly suited to the work of a deacon. His death will leave a void in the church that no one man will be able to fill.

The difference in these two men can be clearly seen in the exhortation of Ecclesiastes 9.10: "Whatever your hand finds to do, do it with your might." What the second man has and the first man lacks is **vision** to see what needs to be done (his hand finds something to do) and **initiative** to do it with his might. These two qualities enable the one to be happy, busy, useful, pleasant, and influential; a lack of them leaves the other miserable, limited, sensitive, stifled by self-pity.

To our many readers who are limited in "leadership" roles we would ask: "Which of these two men present a true picture of you?" Open your eyes! There are needs all about you! Get to work! "There is room in the kingdom…for the small things you can do." Everybody can't be the quarterback; everybody can't be the chief; but everybody can contribute. Let each person find his own role, work diligently in that role, and rejoice in the contribution he can make to the welfare of the Lord's work.

Two Men Are Members of the Same Church

Two men are members of the same local church. That church is involved in a series of gospel meetings and it is Thursday night. **The first man** is present. **The second man** had left that morning on a pleasure trip, having assured the visiting preacher that he would listen to the tape.

The first man worships God on that Thursday night. He is present before God's throne. He sings to God. He praises God. He joins with others in prayer. He expresses thanksgiving to God. He is in fellowship with other Christians for that hour, exhorting and encouraging them and being exhorted and encouraged by them. He worships. He participates. He is involved. He glorifies God.

The second man listens to a tape.

The first man demonstrates that his priorities are right, that he is seeking "first the kingdom of God and His righteousness" (Matt 6.33), that he views the kingdom of heaven as a hidden treasure and as a pearl of great price, to be valued above all earthly pleasures or treasures (Matt 13.44-46). He will not offer to the Lord "that which costs him nothing" (2 Sam 24.24). He is present. He is putting first things first.

The second man listens to a tape.

The first man's actions are encouraging to others. He encourages the preacher, sitting with his Bible open, listening carefully (only a preacher could understand how encouraging a good listener can be), then making some perceptive comment after the lesson. He encourages the song leader, participating heartily in the singing. He encourages the non-Christian, singing the invitation song fervently, sincerely hoping for response. He encourages visitors, speaking to them, chatting for a few minutes, making them feel welcome and inviting them to return. He encourages other members of the congregation. Just in his unfailing attendance at every service he speaks volumes concerning what real faithfulness involves. He has done nothing for show. In fact, as he returns home he has little awareness of the encouragement he has been to many because he was present.

The second man listens to a tape

The first man is a better man for having been present. His faith is stronger. His determination to live for the Lord is greater. He finds joy in knowing that he has made the right decision in how that evening should be spent. He is closer to God and closer to heaven. He is better equipped for the struggles and stresses of the next day.

The second man's pleasure trip is not as enjoyable as he had anticipated. He knows that the meeting is going on at home and that he ought to be there. He has tried to salve his conscience by promising to listen to the tape, but deep down he knows that God is not pleased with his actions. He does listen to the tape, but what a contrast between his actions and those of the first man! What a contrast between the effects the worship period has upon the second man as he listens to his tape and what it had had on the first.

It is not our purpose to discredit a proper use of tapes. They are wonderful. They enable shut-ins to hear sermons that otherwise they could never hear. They enable preachers to extend the influence and teaching of the gospel beyond the bounds of one assembly. They enable travelers in their cars to spend time profitably that otherwise would have been wasted. They reach to Christians in isolated places who otherwise have little opportunity to hear good Bible teaching. They even enable preachers to critique their own lessons (This writer has not just critiqued, but scrapped a few.)

Acceptable worship, however, focuses upon God, not a preacher. Acceptable worship involves participation: "Make a joyful shout to the Lord" (Psa 100.1). There is a social aspect to acceptable worship: "Teaching and admonishing one another..." (Col 3.16). Acceptable worship involves praise and thanksgiving and petition and expressions of dependence. This cannot be done by "audio." Our second man listens to a tape, and receives some information from the sermon, but what he does cannot substitute for true worship, nor can it justify his absence from that Thursday night meeting.

Two Churches Want to Grow

Two churches want to grow, but their attitudes toward growth differ greatly.

The first church looks upon growth as its primary purpose. Goals are placed before the membership: "We want to double our membership within the next three years," for instance. Success (or failure) is judged almost entirely on the basis of that congregation's numerical growth.

The second church looks upon the saving of souls as its primary purpose and any growth in membership is just a natural result of that primary purpose. Members of the second church are infused with the value of immortal souls rather than a sense of congregational pride.

Members of **the first church** become eager to get people to the water. Baptism is the point at which people are added to the membership list; consequently, it's going to take so many baptisms to keep pace with their goal of doubling their membership. They must not only get them to the water, they must get them there within the time period that has been arbitrarily set by their leaders.

Members of **the second church** are far more eager to get people to repent. Their concern is for additions to the Lord's body rather than additions to a membership list. Their approach is to bring sinners to a consciousness of their sin and the consequences of remaining in sin. If they can do this in one study, great! But if considerable time is required to uproot false concepts and to plant the true seed of the gospel, they patiently accept this. Their only sense of urgency grows out of the uncertainty of life and its duration. But they know that shortcuts are not the answer; that baptism without repentance is worthless; and that once people are brought to true repentance, having been properly taught, baptism for the remission of sins will follow. So they wait with longsuffering until the gospel brings about its desired effect in the hearts of those whom they are teaching.

Members of **the first church** will be tempted to use questionable tactics in their approach to people. The old methods and approaches don't seem to be effective any more. New and more positive approaches must be found. So the members of the first church make their appeal to the pride of people. They persuade them of their self-worth; they build their self-image; they tell them how valuable they would be to the congregation. "We need you," they tell their prospects. They might also extol the virtues of the congregation, persuading their prospects of the value of being a part of such a vibrant, growing group of people. So, people "become members," and they conform to the rules that are placed before them for acceptance within the group, but there may have been little grief over sin; in fact, they might even still believe they were Christians before they "became members."

The members of **the second church** recognize that the gospel never makes its appeal to the pride of people. They bring people to see their spiritual bankruptcy; that they have "nothing to pay"; that their true worth is not to be found in self, but in Christ; that they must humble themselves and look to Christ for their exaltation; that they are sinners in desperate need of salvation; that their only hope is to be found in Christ. They would bring them to say, in the words of Mrs. C.H. Morris:

Nearer, still nearer, nothing I bring,
Naught as an offering to Jesus my King,
Only my sinful, now contrite heart;
Grant me the cleansing Thy blood doth impart.

The first church may become compromising in its teaching. Its elders intend to maintain doctrinal soundness, but there is the pressure to produce, to maintain the growth rate set before the congregation. When doctrinal soundness becomes an obstacle to that purpose, the elders may succumb to the pressures and ease up on its teaching. **The second church** faces no such pressure, for in its concern for the spiritual wellbeing of people, there is desire for truth on every subject vital to salvation.

The emphasis of **the first church** is organizational and institutional; the emphasis of the second is spiritual and heavenly.

We commend **the second church** to our readers. Serious problems can result when churches see growth as their primary purpose. If goals are to be set—and goals can serve a good purpose—let them focus on the number to be taught rather than the number to be baptized. If new approaches are needed, let them be conceived only if they are compatible with God's wisdom. In efforts to reach others, let all determine to know nothing "except Jesus Christ and Him crucified." When churches thus become really serious about saving souls, God will give the increase and growth will take care of itself.

Two Ways to Keep Members Faithful

There are two ways to keep members of the church "faithful." **The first way** is to be sure everyone is involved. Have a project for each member, and make sure that he feels important in his role. Praise him for the good job he is doing. Make him feel needed; make him feel that the well-being of the whole congregation rests firmly on his shoulders. That will keep him "faithful."

There are two problems with this method. In the first place, it encourages the creation of projects that are not remotely related to the work of the local church. One member plays on the church ball team; another leads the Boy Scout troop; another is an active member of the "Dorcas Society"; another plans the program for the men's luncheon. Everybody is busy all right, but in activities that are not authorized in the New Testament.

In the second place, members are often given roles for which they are not qualified. A lady is chosen to teach a class, not because she is qualified, but because she needs to be involved. A man is appointed a deacon to help him to be "faithful." Another man is appointed to serve the Lord's Supper for a month in order to encourage him to be present each Sunday that month. This method thus places "the cart before the horse," for no one should ever be assigned any work in the Lord's service who is not already faithful and qualified for the work to be done (2 Tim 2.2).

The second way to keep people faithful is to develop within them a genuine love for the Lord. When people love the Lord, they will be faithful, and it won't take some kind of "special" project to keep them faithful. They will also be involved: in worship, in study, in prayer, in godly living, in sharing the gospel with a friend, in helping the needy. I have known literally hundreds of Christians who have never in their lives been appointed to any special work, but whose love for the Lord alone keeps them faithful. There is no superficial faithfulness on the part of these; theirs is a faithfulness that is real.

Special responsibilities are fine for those who are qualified, but the man who requires some special duty to be faithful has never learned what true faithfulness is.

Two Kings Seek Greatness

Jeremiah speaks of two kings who sought greatness (Jer 22.13-16). **The first king**, Jehoiakim, had an interesting approach: Enlarge your houses, remodel your buildings, paint them with vermilion, surround yourself with luxuries, and show yourself to be a great king. His obvious concept: **Greatness is to be found in externals**. Jeremiah's challenging question to Jehoiakim was: "Do you become a king because you are competing in cedar?" (22.15, NASB).

Jehoiakim's father—**our second king**—had demonstrated a different concept of greatness. Josiah had not neglected "eating and drinking," but he had shown far greater concern for doing justice and righteousness, judging the cause of the afflicted and needy, and coming to know God (22.15-16). His concept had been: **Externals have their place, but true greatness is to be found in justice, compassion, righteousness, humble service to God and man**.

The concept of Jehoiakim can easily make its way into the church. A preacher, wanting to make a name for himself, carefully cultivates just the right connections, develops just the right dress and personality, and begins to make his way toward "greatness." In seeking for a solution to dull, lifeless worship periods, men will change the order of service, dim the lights, encourage "spontaneous" singing, even change hymn books—looking for excellence through manipulating externals. A congregation enlarges the building, redecorates its auditorium, initiates new programs, and develops more modern phraseology to give its programs a ring of sophistication as it reaches for "first class" status in the eyes of men. Borrowing the style of Jeremiah, we ask: Do you become a preacher by fashion, style, and political maneuvering? Do you become a great church because you are competing in brick and mortar? Do you make people spiritual by dimming lights and changing the order of services?

We are not suggesting that externals should be ignored. They have their place. Neatness in appearance and pleasantness of manner can be of some value in a preacher's work. Clean and well-kept buildings and grounds usually reflect diligence in other aspects of a church's work. And the Lord has certainly taught us concerning our worship periods, "Let all things be done decently and in order" (1 Cor 14.40).

But true greatness on the part of a preacher or a church is to be found, not in externals, but in genuineness, humility, knowledge, spirituality, love for truth, concern for the lost, faith, courage, hope, obedience, trust, service to God and man. These are qualities that make for greatness in God's sight. The real solution to dull, lifeless worship periods is to be found in worshipful, grateful, loving worshipers. Change the people, and the worship periods will take care of themselves.

Greatness indeed is to be sought, but let us not confuse the fleeting admiration of fickle and unstable men with true greatness.

Two Elders Oversee

Two men are appointed elders, but they vary greatly as they oversee the flock. **The first man** is a mere spokesman for a small minority of the congregation. He has little contact with anybody beyond his family and closest friends. When he has heard them on some question he thinks he has heard all; their strong approval of any work is interpreted as a mandate from the whole congregation.

The second man is concerned for the entire group. He cultivates friendship with all and values the thinking of the less vocal ones as highly as he does that of his closest friends. In fact, he frequently seeks the advice and thinking of those who are not so quick to speak.

He extends hospitality to all who are a part of the church, but especially to those who might feel neglected or left out of things. He loves every member and finds some way to communicate his love and appreciation for each one.

The first man calls on the same few people for every task to be performed. When he visits the sick or shut-ins, he is always accompanied by these same ones. He is unaware of the spiritual development of those on the "fringe;" in fact, he hardly knows them. If he ever has to go to one of them with a problem, he goes as a stranger rather than as a friend or a brother.

The second man works for the spiritual development of every member. He is aware of young people who have potential and is helping them develop that potential for the Lord's use. He is constantly encouraging men to lead their first prayer or make their first talk. He encourages women who have been hesitant in the past to become involved in teaching, extending hospitality, or preparing a dish for a bereaved family. He knows that good leadership develops leadership in others, and is constantly looking out for those who might serve as elders in the future and lends them encouragement. The best word to describe this man is "awareness." He knows the people and they know him. Their problems are his problems; their sorrows, his sorrows; their joys, his joys. He is aware of their potential, their strengths, their weaknesses, their needs.

The first man can actually be a hindrance to the welfare of the church and a major frustration to the purposes and goals of the second man. Elders have the responsibility of mixing with the whole group and to act impartially. They must consider the **needs** of all rather than the selfish **desires** of the few. They must "watch for the souls" of all (Heb 13.17).

It is obvious that it is **the second man** in our article who pleases God as an elder. In fact, our article might best be entitled, "One Elder Oversees," for our first man does more "overlooking" than "overseeing;" more resting in the sheepfold than pastoring the flock. "Therefore take heed to yourselves and to all the flock…" (Acts 20.28).

Two Churches Have Elders

Two churches have elders, but they differ tremendously in their attitudes toward the elders. **The first church** sees the elders as great targets for criticism. Every move is questioned, and much discontent and unrest exist. In fact, the elders have to spend so much time dealing with the unrest that they have little time to plan and implement work that will bring the church to fulfillment of its God-given purpose.

The second church recognizes the heavy load borne by the elders, and they are thankful that there are men who are willing to do the work. They make allowances for their imperfections and seek to be supportive in every way possible. If a decision is made that some member believes to be unwise, he goes to the elders with his problem and does not stir unrest within the congregation. The members are "ready to do every good work," willing to cooperate in any activity that is in keeping with God's authority.

The first church thinks of the elders as mere decision makers. They resent the elders' effort to admonish. They view any attempt to talk with someone about sin in his life as an intrusion into his privacy. They really wish the elders would just make whatever decisions they have to make and leave everybody alone.

The second church recognizes that in their role as shepherds, the elders must make certain decisions pertaining to the welfare of the church, but they see them primarily as "watchers for souls" and spiritual nourishment. They respect the elders and respond to their admonitions. They know that the prodding is for their good and that the elders have their spiritual and eternal welfare in mind.

The members of **the first church** rarely express appreciation for their elders and rarely pray for them. They see their elders' faults but are blinded to their good traits. There is not that good elder-congregation relationship that God desires in His church. Some of the faults may lie with the elders themselves, but the congregation has really not given them the chance to rule and exercise oversight that should be theirs.

The second church is an example of peace and harmony. They appreciate their elders, pray for them, and "esteem them very highly in love for their work's sake" (1 Thes 5.12-13). They frequently express to them their love and support, so that the elders work among them with confidence, fulfilling their heavy responsibilities "with joy and not with grief" (Heb 13.17).

The first church wonders why they can't have a strong eldership like that of the second church, never realizing that the response of the congregation itself determines to a great extent the effectiveness with which the elders oversee, lead, and rule the church. The key to change in the first church lies within just a few, who, with a change in their own attitudes, could lead the whole group into better attitudes. Could it be possible that **you** are among that few?

Three Men Present the Word

How positive and certain should one be in his presentation of the word? We have observed three types of men in relation to this question.

The first is the mealy-mouthed type who rarely says anything with certainty. Every statement is prefaced with "possibly," "it could be," "some of the commentaries say," or "I think." Even Revelation 21.8: "But the cowardly, unbelieving…and all liars shall have their part in the lake which burns with fire and brimstone…." is quoted in soft, suave tones (and that requires real skill!) that will convince no one.

The second voices everything in a positive, self-assured way, especially those proclamations about which he knows absolutely nothing. He can be wrong in the most positive kind of way. He is the true dogmatist, living by the philosophy, "Yell here; point's weak;" or possibly he is self-deceived, failing to recognize his limitations.

The third studies very closely the word of the Lord, and consequently speaks with certainty those conclusions which he can defend from the scriptures. When he speaks, the listener is impressed that "this man really believes what he is saying." He is not afraid of being questioned on any conviction, for he is "always…ready to give a defense to everyone who asks [him] a reason for the hope that is in [him], with meekness and fear" (1 Pet 3.15). At the same time, he is not hesitant to say, "I don't know," when questioned about a matter of which he is not certain.

Of these three types, the second is the most unacceptable and the most dangerous. We marvel at the brazenness of such men, but marvel even more at the gullibility of congregations who will allow them to dominate their classes, pulpits, and business meetings.

On the other hand, the person who allows his repulsion to the second type drive him to an acceptance of the wishy-washy, "never be certain of anything" type, makes a sad mistake. Truth has its own peculiar ring, and that ring is the ring of certainty. One hears it unmistakably in the teaching of the apostles: "I know whom I have believed…" (2 Tim 1.12); "For we did not follow cunningly devised fables…" (2 Pet 1.16); "We also believe and therefore speak, knowing…" (2 Cor 4.13-14). And one will hear it in faithful teaching today.

Truth is the deciding factor. When one can support his teaching with a proper application of scripture, he can—no; he should—speak with boldness, clarity, and certainty. Such teaching is not dogmatism; it is contending "earnestly for the faith." It should not be criticized; it should be appreciated and encouraged. Let no one then be intimidated, "For God has not given us a spirit of fear, but of power and of love and of a sound mind. Therefore do not be ashamed of the testimony of our Lord…" (2 Tim 1.7-8).

Two Men Teach God's Word

People who are useful in the Lord's service are balanced in their thinking. They maintain moderation of the mind. They know what they believe and why they believe it, and are not given to radical fluctuations of thought.

Two men are teachers of God's word. Both are conscientious men who love truth. **The first man**, however, is easily swayed by whatever he reads and hears. He frequently changes positions on doctrinal issues. Wanting to be independent in his thinking, he is quick to reject traditional "Church of Christ" thinking. He adopts into his thinking anything that on the surface sounds reasonable to him. He loves to come across some new, exciting "gem" that will set his teaching apart from the old, stale teaching that people have heard for years. Above all, he wants his teaching to be thought-provoking and challenging, different and exciting, new and fresh in its approach.

The second man wants his teaching to be challenging and thought-provoking, too, but he recognizes that one does not have to reject that which is tried and proven in order to be challenging and independent. He is not surprised to find that his convictions are similar to those of others who have labored to separate error from truth, traditionalism from the pure word of God, sectarianism from the unity found in Christ. After all, he shares the same goals and studies the same book. He sees no virtue in being different from them. He has come to solid conclusions based on his study of the scriptures and is not easily swayed from those conclusions. He finds truth challenging because it is truth.

The first man tends to be "tossed to and fro and carried about with every wind of doctrine" (Eph 4.14). His hearers never know what to expect from him next. One thing they can be sure of: whatever "kick" he is on at the time will come out in his lessons, for every new concept seems to become an obsession.

The second man has his heart "established by grace" (Heb 13.9); he is "grounded and steadfast" (Col 1.23). He questions positions he has held, and is forced by his own personal honesty and integrity to change positions occasionally, but he acts very slowly and cautiously in doing so. He keeps many questions that arise in his mind to himself, for he recognizes that they are not vital to his own salvation or to the salvation of others.

The first man unnecessarily disturbs others with his teaching, leaving them with more questions than answers. Some of his conclusions are dangerous. And though he later recognizes their danger and discards them, he has already, in his haste, planted seeds of error in the hearts of his hearers. His influence is hurt because brethren are afraid of him—justifiably afraid. His usefulness in the kingdom is greatly affected.

We would suggest to our **first man** that before he creates trouble among God's people and hurts his own influence, he might ask the following questions.

1. Am I sure of the conclusions I have reached? Is it possible that I have overlooked some pertinent scripture or argument that would negate my conclusions?

2. Am I sure that my conclusions have not been tainted by prejudice, disillusionment, bitterness, jealousy, emotional considerations, or some other factor that can adversely affect one's thinking?

3. Even if I am sure of my conclusions, is the point I am stressing vital, of sufficient importance to justify problems?

4. Have I allowed these conclusions to become an obsession? Do I find myself talking about them frequently—in Bible classes? In sermons? In private discussions? Do I find my reading of the Scriptures somewhat "colored" by these new concepts?

We are not encouraging compromise, nor are we suggesting that one must gain brotherhood approval for his conclusions before teaching them. We are saying, however, that caution dictates that one go slowly in adopting new concepts and be even more cautious in teaching them. "Let your gentleness be known to all men" (Phil 4.5)

Two Men Preach the Gospel

Faithful preaching of the gospel demands a certain amount of negative teaching. The evils of immorality, doctrinal error, and division must be shown. Internal problems must be dealt with. But there is a difference between negative preaching and negativism. For instance…

Two men preach the gospel. **The first man**, however, is given to negativism. Practically all of his sermons are either an expose of some false doctrine or a denunciation of the congregation for its weaknesses. Members attend worship periods wondering "what he's going to fuss about today?" While he may not intend for it to be so, his basic message to the congregation is, "You aren't! You can't! You won't!"

The second man recognizes the necessity of negative teaching, too, but his overall approach is positive. He looks ahead to the goals he believes the church can attain, and he plans his lessons with those goals in mind. He seeks to do his part in bringing every member to a closer relationship with God, to a greater faith in prayer, to a greater love for one another, to a greater desire for heaven. He also wants to bring each member to a hatred for sin and false teaching, and his negative teaching is presented with this in mind. When sin raises its ugly head in the congregation, he knows how to rebuke, even sharply. But his basic message to the congregation is, "You are! You can! I know you will!"

The first man just cannot understand why so many criticize his preaching. "They cannot endure the sound doctrine," he thinks. And he argues his case well: "Wasn't the Lord negative in His denunciation of the scribes and Pharisees (Matt 23)?" he asks. "And what about His letters to the Ephesians (Rev 2.1-7) and to the Laodiceans (Rev 3.14-22)?" Having so reasoned, he is sure that his preaching is not the problem; that the problem lies elsewhere.

The second man recognizes that Jesus frequently spoke negatively (sometimes with a finality comparable to that which we might express concerning false teachers of our day—Matt 15.12-14; 21.28-46), but that His overall teaching was a sensitive combination of the negative with instruction, hope, concern, and reassurance. He hears the denunciations, too, but he also hears the Lord's appeals to the denounced, "O Jerusalem, Jerusalem…" (Matt 23.37), "To him who overcomes…" (Rev 2.7), and "Behold, I stand at the door and knock…" (Rev 3.20). Seeking to pattern his own teaching after the Lord's, he strives for the proper balance between the negative and the positive. He holds out hope to others. He constantly points them to a merciful Savior who forgives His true followers.

The first man discourages others, while **the second man** touches the lives of many for good. Both men are sincere, but the first merely tears down the evil, while the second tears down the evil **and** builds the good.

Three Men Preach the Gospel

Three men preach the gospel. **Tom** is the "rant and rave" type. He gets so "worked up" in his preaching. Sweat pours as he speaks excitedly of the Lord and His gospel. His personality is the same outside the pulpit. He is very outgoing and makes friends easily. Tom is well-liked, and is working very effectively for the Lord.

Dick is so different from Tom. He is very conversational in his preaching. His sermons develop more slowly than do Tom's, but there is warmth in his presentation, and one almost gets the impression that Dick is talking directly to him. Dick, too, is effective, both in and out of the pulpit, as a servant of the Lord.

Harry is still different from the other two. His is the more scholarly type of preaching. Subject matter stands out above style or presentation. He is harder to listen to than the other two men, but the careful listener leaves the service well rewarded. His thinking has been challenged. He has had his "bucket" filled. Believe it or not, Harry is effective, too, and is in constant demand among the churches.

This writer must admit that Dick is his favorite type of preacher; that is, until he hears Tom; and then Tom is his favorite type until he hears Harry. It just seems to depend on which one he's listening to at the moment as to which is his favorite style or favorite preacher. But he must admit, too, that there are some preachers he just has trouble listening to. They don't appeal to him very much. And yet, the very preacher that doesn't appeal to this writer may be someone else's favorite. Men differ so greatly in style, in personality, in delivery, in subject matter, in voice, and even in ability. But every faithful preacher is somebody's favorite preacher, for just as preachers vary in their preaching, listeners vary in what they like in preachers.

The Corinthians apparently couldn't appreciate different types of preachers. Partyism resulted. "I am of Paul," they said; or "I am of Apollos," or "I am of Cephas," or "I am of Christ" (1 Cor 1.12). Can you imagine it? Here are four great characters, one of whom is the Son of God; but three must be rejected because the Corinthians have room in their hearts for only one. How badly they needed to enlarge their hearts to be genuinely thankful for every good man and every good influence that had touched their lives. "Therefore let no man boast in men. For all things are yours: whether Paul or Apollos or Cephas, or the world or life or death, or things present or things to come—all are yours. And you are Christ's, and Christ is God's" (1 Cor 3.21-23).

Preachers must find the role in which they can do their most effective work. Elders must find men who can best meet the needs of the congregation. But let us all be thankful for every good man who faithfully proclaims the gospel of Christ.

Two Men View Their Lost Neighbor

Two men view their lost neighbor, but they see him from different perspectives. **The first man** sees him as a potential asset to the church. For years, the church with which he worships has struggled for want of manpower and leadership, and here's the very man who could fill the void. "If we could only win him over," the first man thinks, "what a help he could be to us."

The second man sees him primarily as one in need of salvation. He sees him as one who is lost, without Christ now, and doomed for hell eternally. True, the man could be an asset to the church if he was genuinely converted, but his need for Christ and salvation is infinitely greater than the church's need for him. "If we can bring him to Christ," the second man thinks," he can be saved, go to heaven, and bring glory to the Lord."

The first man approaches the neighbor, telling him how much the church needs him and what an asset he could be. His appeal is built upon flattery and pride.

The second man approaches him with the gospel. He tries to bring him to an awareness of his sinfulness, hopelessness, and helplessness. He points him to Christ as the only answer to his greatest need. He knows that until this man is shaken from his lofty opinion of self, he cannot come to Christ; that until he comes with poverty of spirit, mourning, meekness, hungering, and thirsting for righteousness, etc., he cannot have salvation or be fit for the Master's use. His appeal is therefore built upon persuasion and urgent conviction.

The first man would have his neighbor come down the aisle with a smile on his face to do the church a favor. **The second man** would have him come with bitter tears seeking that which he so desperately needs. The first man's concept of the church is primarily that of an organization seeking help for its basic needs. The second man's concept is that of people who have bowed in submission to Christ and have found in Him the answer to their needs. The first man's appeal is carnal; the second man's appeal is spiritual. The first man may be successful in getting his neighbor "into the church" and "winning him over," but the second man will be successful in saving a soul from death. Unfortunately, the first man may "win" more with his approach than the second man, for the carnal appeal seems far stronger than the spiritual in our day, but, in truth, he weakens the church with everyone he "converts."

"The weapons of our warfare are not carnal but mighty in God for pulling down strongholds" (2 Cor 10.4). These mighty weapons must be used skillfully, but there is no room for substitutes. Fleshly appeals must be cast aside. Flattery and pride represent the very opposite spirit from that of the Lord's kingdom. Indeed, our second man uses the only approach that is pleasing to God.

Two Men Became Preachers

Two men became preachers. **The first man** approached the work solely from a professional viewpoint. He had observed several things about the life of a preacher that had appealed to him. He liked the idea of standing before audiences every week, and for thirty minutes being "the center of attention;" he liked the compliments and the kind words of encouragement; he had observed the rise in preachers' salaries; and he especially hoped to preach in meetings and to be well-known in the brotherhood; he had noticed that preachers were "looked up to," and were often entertained in the homes of the brethren. These were the primary incentives that had led him to become a preacher.

The second man had given little thought to becoming a preacher. He had just worked hard to be a Christian, to be the kind of person with whom God would be pleased. But the elders, impressed with his dedication and good life, had asked him to speak one Sunday evening, and thus he had begun. Soon other churches had learned of his abilities, and they, too, had invited him to speak. Finally a conflict had developed between his pressing secular duties and the time being spent in the Lord's work, and a choice had to be made: either give up his secular work or turn down opportunities to work for the Lord. His love for the Lord would not allow the latter, so after much thought; he gave up his job to go "full time" in the preaching of the gospel. His only incentive was his love for souls and desires to please the Lord.

The first man soon became rather disillusioned. He found that the brethren didn't bow to every whim of the preacher as he had thought they did, and he was especially incensed when one of the brethren questioned something he had said in a Bible class. Besides, the articles he had sent in to "the brotherhood papers" were not even printed, and after five years of preaching he still hadn't been asked to preach in a meeting. Some of his friends were by now preaching for the bigger churches and were receiving considerable publicity, and this led him to greater discouragement. Eventually, an opportunity for secular employment was presented to him, and he took it. He continued to attend services of the church, but bitterness and resentment remained. He was the tragic victim of professionalism in the pulpit.

The second man, "having put his hand to the plow," never looked back. He preached wherever opportunities presented themselves—in big places, in small places; in dwellings, in tents; to the rich, to the poor; to the educated, to the uneducated; when there was support, when there was no support. And whenever he preached, he thanked God for using him in spite of his unworthiness. He never achieved fame, but then he never sought for fame. When he died, he left behind thousands of souls who had been moved by his influence, and he went "home" to that eternal reward for which he had devoted his life.

"My brethren, let not many of you become teachers, knowing that we shall receive a stricter judgment" (Jas 3.1).

Two Preachers View Their Work

Two preachers vary greatly in their attitudes toward their work. **The first preacher** feels that he should be in the pulpit whenever the church assembles for "worship periods" and should teach a class during every Bible study period, while the **second preacher** encourages others to speak and frequently sits in Bible classes taught by others. Their differing actions grow out of two different philosophies as to how churches develop.

The first preacher believes that the greatest development comes from having the "best" to preach and teach. He has studied hard and is truly the best-informed man in the congregation; he is paid to preach; he must, therefore, be the best-qualified for the work; consequently, he should do the preaching and teaching. He guards his "position" in the pulpit and classroom very carefully. Surrender of either comes with great reluctance. "After all, why should the church be forced to listen to men of inferior ability when I could be doing the instructing?" he asks himself.

The second preacher believes the greatest development of the whole comes when each individual is given the opportunity to develop. It is his goal to bring the congregation to less dependence on "the full-time preacher" rather than to greater dependence on him; to develop abilities within others rather than to stifle their development. He recognizes, too, that he is not the only one who has thoughts that the congregation needs to hear; that a different approach can be instructive and refreshing, and especially when it comes from the lips of one who may relate to the congregation better than "the full-time preacher." It is not that he is lazy and does not want to teach. He has spent his life trying to become an effective teacher, and, frankly, it is easier for him to teach than not to teach, to preach than not to preach; but he sits, sometimes agonizingly, while others are given a chance to develop and instruct. He does so because he is persuaded that the overall strength of the church will be served by bringing others into the teaching program.

It may "boil down" to a question of judgment, but we agree with the second preacher's philosophy. We would not turn the worship periods of the church into mere training sessions (training classes should be provided for beginners), but as men develop in their abilities to edify the church, they should be allowed to speak and to share their thoughts with the congregation. And it ought to be the goal of preachers and elders to bring men to be able to edify. Further, the church should be brought to acceptance of such men in the pulpit and classroom. Churches do not become strong by one man doing all the preaching and teaching.

Good leadership develops leadership in others. Effective preaching develops others who are capable of preaching (2 Tim 2.2). And we are persuaded that it is the second preacher who will accomplish these purposes, not the first.

Two Preachers Talk Money

Two preachers hold opposite viewpoints concerning money. **The first** believes that when he goes to talk with a congregation about working with them, he should get all he can out of that congregation right then, for surely he will never get anything out of them after he moves. **The second** believes that brethren have a pretty good idea as to what a man needs to live and support his family, so he takes more of a "low-key" type of approach. He is frank concerning his needs, but is not demanding.

The first man is absolutely right in his evaluation of congregations. He **can't** get anything out of them after he moves. They have already observed his money-hungry (we dare not call it "covetous") disposition; they have already been drained of everything he can get out of them; and they are not about to give him more. Money becomes a touchy subject. The preacher resents the "tight strings" policy of the church. The church resents the preacher's desire for more money. Everywhere he goes he faces the same problem. He writes and talks constantly of the selfishness of churches. The churches look upon him more and more as a "professional," although he will probably be the last to know.

The second man receives less support than the first at moving time, but he usually finds congregations appreciative of his "low-key" approach and considerate of his financial needs. He is occasionally offered a raise which he may or may not accept, depending on his own needs and the ability of the congregation to furnish the raise. Oh, he sometimes finds himself working for a church that is not as considerate as it ought to be, but he is determined that if the church doesn't support him in keeping with his mind, he'll just bring his mind down in keeping with the support. A little more care in long-distance telephone calling, restaurant dining, out-of-town traveling, and clothes buying (the preacher doesn't have to be the style setter) works wonders for his budget. All in all, he comes out quite well financially, and is spared the money conflicts that the first preacher has with every congregation with which he labors. Even as he grows older and faces periods of less activity, he enjoys a peculiar sense of financial security in his faith in God's providence coupled with the love and esteem which have resulted from his unselfish devotion to the cause and will be demonstrated even in monetary ways.

We suppose it is unnecessary to state which viewpoint is advocated by the writer. There are hundreds of other preachers who share his viewpoint. We have no sympathy for the stingy, unthoughtful churches. But neither do we have sympathy for preachers who are always crying about money. After all, it was to a preacher that the following words were written: "For the love of money is a root of all kinds of evil, for which some have strayed from the faith in their greediness, and pierced themselves through with many sorrows. But you, O man of God, flee these things ..." (1 Tim 6.10-11).*

*Please see page number 149 to read an article that gives balance to this one.

Two Men Disagree With the Preacher

Two men disagree with the preacher. They have both been taught that they are not just to "swallow" everything the preacher says; that they are to think for themselves. They are to be commended, therefore, for their careful evaluation of what is taught.

The key words with **the first man**, however, are, "It seems to me." All teaching is judged according to his own thinking, as to whether or not it makes sense to him.

The key words with **the second man** are, "What does God say about it?" He desires truth and knows that truth can only be found in God's word (John 17.17). If he disagrees with the preacher, he does so because he is convinced the preacher has misused a passage of scripture or has failed to consider a scripture that might affect his conclusion. He comes with an open Bible and an open mind, prepared to defend his position or to yield if he sees that it is indefensible.

The first man exalts self. He places too much confidence in his own thinking. He may do so unconsciously, but in reality he makes his own intellect and experiences his god. His thinking is reflected in the words of Naaman, "Behold, I thought," words that would have taken Naaman to a leper's grave had it not been for the admonition of his servants (2 Kgs 5.1-14).

The second man exalts God. His confidence is in what God says in the scriptures. He recognizes that his own intellect and experience fade, into nothingness when placed in the brightness of the light of truth. A "thus saith the Lord" ends all controversy with him. His thinking is reflected in that of the Bereans who "were more fair-minded than those in Thessalonica, in that they…searched the Scriptures daily to find out whether these things were so" (Acts 17.11).

Unless **the first man** changes his attitude he is hopeless. He is susceptible to all manner of false ideas. He cannot come to know God and His truth through his own wisdom (1 Cor 1.21). He must throw his own wisdom, intellect, and experience aside; he must become poor in spirit, meek before God, mourning, hungering and thirsting for righteousness; he must bow in submission to the Lord and to His word. He must say with Paul, "Oh, the depth of the riches both of the wisdom and knowledge of God! How unsearchable are His judgments and His ways past finding out! 'For who has known the mind of the LORD? Or who has become His counselor?'" (Rom 11.33-34).

The second man is a blessed and fortunate man indeed, for he will learn the truth that will make him free (John 8.32). Unfortunately, he is a rare man in the twentieth century. But he does exist—and he can exist even in the man who is presently reading this article. What a challenge to each of us! After all, it is one thing to disagree with a preacher, but quite another thing to disagree with Almighty God!

Two Women Were Married To Non-Christians

Two women were married to non-Christians.

The first woman remembered that she was to love the Lord, even above her own husband (Luke 14.26), and determined in her heart that she would be faithful to the Lord. She never missed a service of the church just to be with her husband. She never compromised her principles to engage in some questionable activity with him. At the same time she never gave her husband reason to question her love; in fact, he could see that her faithfulness to the Lord led her to be in subjection to him, to love him, to satisfy his physical needs, to be the best wife and mother she could possibly be. She was always loyal to her husband until conflicts arose between her loyalty to him and her loyalty for Christ. She prayed constantly for him and expressed to him her concern for his soul, but she determined not to nag him constantly about obeying the gospel.

The second woman's concept was completely different. She had often heard those scriptures about loving the Lord above everything else, but she didn't want to offend her husband. "After all," she thought, "if I go to every service and am constantly leaving my husband at home alone, he will soon hate the church, and will never become a Christian." She carefully shielded him from the preacher or anyone who might want to talk with him, and even sometimes went with him to places where Christians should never go. She thought that if she did some things that he wanted to do, then possibly, he might do some things that she wanted to do, like go to services.

The husband of **the first woman** observed the true value of serving the Lord. He could see the joy, the peace, the strength which was hers through Christ. He appreciated the good people with whom she worshiped. He began to read some of the tracts and Bible material which were brought home from the services and eventually began attending some of the services with his wife. He resisted for a while, but gradually the power of the gospel broke down that resistance until on a Sunday evening, as the congregation sang "Oh! Why Not Tonight?" he stepped into the aisle, prepared to render obedience to the gospel.

The husband of **the second woman** was never very impressed with the church. He knew that it meant very little to his wife. And it never occurred to him that she might want him to be a Christian. The wife herself grew weaker and weaker, and although she never completely quit attending, she found little joy in the Lord.

We would not imply that every faithful woman will be successful in converting her husband. But the following instructions from the Lord should be considered, for they contain the Lord's teaching to women whose husbands are not Christians: "Wives, likewise, be submissive to your own husbands, that even if some do not obey the word, they, without a word, may be won by the conduct of their wives, when they observe your chaste conduct accompanied by fear" (1 Pet 3.1-2).

Three Views of Modesty

Three women face the problem of modesty. All three recognize the teaching of 1 Timothy 2.9: "In like manner also, that the women adorn themselves in modest apparel, with propriety and moderation, not with braided hair or gold or pearls or costly clothing ..." but their attitudes toward modesty differ considerably.

The first woman takes the "**Where do you draw the line?**" view. If someone could draw the line for her (at the knee? ankle? calf?) and prove by the Bible that it was the line separating modesty from immodesty, she would abide by it (she says). But, meanwhile, until someone comes up with the Bible line, she wears what she wants to. If anyone approaches her about her immodesty, she justifies herself with one question, "Where do you draw the line?" followed by one observation, "Grandma wore her dress at the ankles, you know."

The second woman takes the "**follow the dress code**" view. She has listened to sermons on modesty, and has established for herself a code of dress by which she lives religiously: no shorts, no halters, no swimsuit, skirt below the knee, high neck, etc. She is a good woman and is to be commended for her conscientiousness, but it has never "dawned" on her that a woman can dress by her code and still be worldly, suggestive, and immodest in appearance. She would be shocked to learn that reasonable people consider her to be immodest at times.

The third woman is concerned about dress, but is more concerned about the **character** of which dress is a reflection. Recognizing Bible teaching concerning purity and chastity, she has become genuinely pure and chaste, not only in conduct, but in heart and disposition. She is pure "through and through," "inside and outside," and her clothing reflects that purity. Decency of dress is not a mechanical, "follow a dress code" type of thing with her. It is a natural outgrowth of her modesty from within. While other sisters in Christ grope with 1 Timothy 2.9 and wonder why the Lord would be so restrictive in their dress, she sees that teaching as being perfectly natural, an obvious supplement to Bible teaching concerning purity and chastity of heart and life.

Her dress reflects her character in other areas. For instance, she seeks to be ladylike in heart and demeanor, and this attitude is reflected in her dress. She remembers the warnings in the scriptures concerning pride, and has become truly "poor in spirit." This is also reflected in her dress. Her dress is a commentary on her character. One glance reveals that here is a woman who is pure, ladylike, and genuine.

And is this not what 1 Timothy 2.9 is teaching? The verse says that we are to dress with modesty, shamefacedness, and sobriety. When we all develop these qualities in our hearts, then, and only then, will our problems of dress vanish.

Two Parents Raise Their Children

Which is worse? A parent who totally dominates the lives and thinking of his children or a parent who places no restrictions upon his children, allowing them to do whatever they please? There may be no legitimate answer to the question. Each is making a sad mistake.

The first parent does not teach his children responsibility. Because he makes all their decisions for them, his children never learn how to make decisions for themselves. Because he tells them every move they are to make, he robs them of individual initiative. Because he gets them up and sees to it that they are on time for every event, they never learn the value of promptness on their own. Because he answers every question for them rather than leading them in finding answers for themselves, he takes from them the ability to think and come to logical conclusions. The first parent's children, in their late teens or early twenties, will find themselves facing a world for which they are poorly prepared. In their immaturity they will be vulnerable to the domination of others, and in some cases it will be those who would destroy them.

But **the second parent** makes a sad mistake, too. He forces his children into decisions that they are not sufficiently mature to make; he allows them to get into situations that they are not capable of handling. "A child left to himself brings shame to his mother" (Prov 29.15).

Children need parents who will teach them right and wrong. They need to learn early in life what "no" means and to have each "no" reinforced with proper discipline. Children must be trained in the way they should go (Prov 22.6). They must be brought "up in the training and admonition of the Lord" (Eph 6.4).

The fruits of permissiveness can be seen in Adonijah, David's son, of whom it is said, "His father had not rebuked him at any time by saying, 'Why have you done so?'" (1 Kgs 1.6). Adonijah had always done what he wanted to do with no restraint from his father. It should not be surprising, therefore, to find him usurping the throne, doing what he wanted to do, even though God had chosen Solomon as David's successor.

The fruits of permissiveness can also be seen in Eli's sons. "His sons made themselves vile and he did not restrain them" (1 Sam 3.13). If Eli was not restraining his sons at this point in their lives, he likely had never restrained them. Their vulgar and immoral lives were the outgrowth of their father's permissiveness.

Parents, then, need to find balance between too much domination and too much permissiveness. We would make the following suggestions:

1. **Set boundaries for your children between what they are allowed to do and what they are forbidden to do.** Make sure the children know where the boundaries are. Maintain the boundaries consistently.

2. **Allow your children to move freely within the boundaries.** If you learn that they have stepped outside the boundaries, respond with firm and appropriate discipline. "Correct your son and he will give you rest; yes, he will give delight to your soul" (Prov 29.17).

3. **As the children grow older, bring them to see that the boundaries that have been set are not really parents' boundaries, but God's.** Speak often of God when your children are young. "And these words which I command you today shall be in your heart. You shall teach them diligently to your children" (Deut 6.6-7). Build into them a desire to please God, reinforced by a fear of stepping outside the boundaries.

4. **Begin to "loosen the apron strings" as the children become more mature and more capable of making decisions.** Hold them responsible for their misconduct. Don't relieve them too quickly of the consequences of poor decisions. After all, we learned from our mistakes, and they must be allowed to do so, too. Place trust in them. Express confidence in their desire to do right. Let them know that you have high expectations of them.

5. **Never, never give permission to do wrong.** Your children will probably do wrong on occasions, but they must always know that Dad and Mother would be hurt badly if they were to learn of it. Never defend your children when they are wrong. Do defend them when they are right. Never give them reason to question your love for them.

6. **Pray that God will somehow overrule your mistakes,** for you will not perform your task perfectly. Then thank Him for His grace and rejoice in your children's growth and spiritual development.

Two Teenagers Struggle for Maturity

Two teenagers struggle for maturity. **The first** has been brought up from childhood to recognize that there is a dark side; that there are failures as well as successes; that there are sacrifices and disappointments to be experienced as well as joys. While his parents have done what they could to cushion the blows of life, they have allowed their child to gradually learn that the blows are there and to be schooled by experience to cope with them when they come.

The second teenager has been carefully shielded from the darker realities of life. He has never been in a funeral home, has never attended a funeral, and has never visited a person with a terminal illness. His parents have taught him little about sacrificing for the Lord. Whenever conflicts have arisen between his own activities of interest and the Lord's work, they have made the decision for him, and being over-solicitous for their child's happiness, they have allowed him to forsake the Lord's work for his own pleasure. He has never even had the decision explained to him or been allowed a choice. He has been granted practically every material request by parents who can't bear to see their child disappointed.

The first teenager has a considerable jump on the second in the maturing process. Decisions involving priorities are easy for him, for he has been making them with the help of parental guidance since childhood. Temptations are still difficult and the desires of the flesh are strong, but, after all, he has never been able to have everything he wanted. He is far better able to "roll with the punches" that life serves up, for he has had some training along those lines. Sickness and death are a reality to him, and he does not feel uncomfortable in their presence. In short, he loves success and joy, but can live with failure and sadness.

The second teenager struggles greatly. He is suddenly taken from his sheltered, unreal environment, and is plunged into a cruel world for which he is unprepared. He is angered and bitter when others fail to cater to him. He is devastated by the "raw deal" he gets on his job. He feels very uncomfortable when death is discussed and shrinks back from the reality of it. He cannot be content on his anemic salary, but when his parents step in to help him finance his accustomed lifestyle, his self-respect is dealt a severe blow. He flounders. He tries "to find himself." And, worse yet, his soul is in danger, for he has never learned to sort out his priorities or to make decisions that are essential for spiritual well-being.

This writer once asked a respected friend how to build strength of character into one's children. The friend's only reply was, "I don't know, but it's not by giving them everything they want." Is it possible, that in our great "love" for our children we have become their worst enemies?

Two Girls Want to Date Jerry

Jerry is a bright young man with a great future. He is a Christian, genuinely dedicated to pleasing the Lord and preparing for heaven. Two girls recognize these great qualities and want to date Jerry, but their approach is considerably different.

The first girl tries to attract Jerry by worldly means. She relies on her physical beauty and "up-to-date" wardrobe. She turns on her charm anytime he is around and is quite forward in his presence. She owns her own car and seeks to use that cherished commodity to the greatest possible advantage. She is a member of the church and attends regularly, but material values obviously outweigh spiritual values in her life. She has some good qualities, but she is placing so much emphasis on outward appearance that it is difficult for one to penetrate the veneer to see her real character.

The second girl makes no obvious effort to attract Jerry at all, for her "meek and quiet spirit" could never allow her to be forward or flirtatious. In her effort to please God, she seeks to develop spiritual qualities in her life, and she would like to think that these spiritual qualities would make her attractive to a spiritual young man. Because she is Christ-like, she is warm, friendly, sympathetic, concerned, the kind of person one can feel close to, and she manifests these qualities in Jerry's presence as she does toward all her acquaintances. She does not possess the physical beauty of the first girl, but she is neat and wholesome in appearance and possesses a beauty from within, which "is very precious in the sight of God" (1 Pet 3.4).

Which girl is Jerry most likely to date? We are not sure. We have seen good boys who, flattered by the attention of flirtatious girls, have made poor choices. And Jerry could make that mistake. But, knowing Jerry, we are quite sure that he will distinguish the girl who will make a great date from the one who will make a great wife, and will choose the latter.

Two vital questions remain to be asked. Girls, which one of the two girls correctly depicts you? Boys, which would you choose for a date? Young people who love the Lord choose mates who will help them to go to heaven.

A Man's Watch—A Man's Life

I watched the man as he opened his gift, a beautiful Seiko watch—digital, calendar, alarm, everything—everything, that is, except for the tranquilizers he needed after futilely trying to set the thing, Poor man—all day long he was punching this button and that button until he complained about his sore finger. The next day he headed for work with his new Seiko watch to see if anyone at work knew how to set it. Of course in the box, lying totally ignored and unobserved was the set of instructions that in simple steps told how to set the watch. But the man preferred to try to figure it out for himself.

What a man does with his watch is of no great significance. But many people tragically do with their lives what that man did with his watch. They seek here and seek there; they experiment with one religion, then another; they question parents, educators, preachers, friends; they read all the literature available; doing all of these things in their futile quest for fellowship with God and eternal life in heaven. Meanwhile, lying on the table beside them, ignored and unobserved, is the Bible, God's instructions for eternal life and happiness.

"Your word," David said, "is a lamp to my feet and a light to my path" (Psa 119.105). God's word provides instructions concerning salvation, morals, human relations, family life, worship, spirituality, fellowship. It has the power to transform miserable wretches into happy and useful servants of the Lord. It can bring the willing person to faith and hope and love. God's word is truth (John 17.17). It furnishes the man of God *for every good* work" (2 Tim 3.16-17). How tragic to see it ignored by the very people who in so many other ways are seeking for life and immortality.

But, back to my friend. He may figure out all on his own how to set that watch. He's pretty clever with such things. But God **in His wisdom** provided a way of salvation which no man can discover through his own wisdom and ingenuity. This is the meaning of 1

Corinthians 1.21: "For since, in the wisdom of God, the world through wisdom did not know God, it pleased God through the foolishness of the message preached to save those who believe." If one is to come to Christ, he must deny himself, remove from consideration what seems reasonable to him, and humbly accept God's word and follow His instructions, even when the entire world views it as "foolishness." This is the reason why "not many wise according to the flesh, not many mighty, not many noble, are called" (1 Cor 1.26), while the "common people" hear Him gladly (Mark 12.37). The common people are just not as likely to try to figure it out for themselves.

We must take the guesswork out of serving the Lord, and learn from His instruction book what we must do. "It is not in man who walks to direct his own steps" (Jer 10.23). Eternity is at stake.

The Scriptures Are Our Guide

Two different views exist as to how one comes to a knowledge of God's will. The first view is that one comes to this knowledge by carefully reading and understanding the scriptures; that Jesus promised His **apostles** that they would be led into all **truth** by the Spirit (John 14.26; 16.13); that they, along with other inspired men, wrote that **truth** in the scriptures; that when we **read** what they wrote, we may "**understand** [their] knowledge in the mystery of Christ" (Eph 3.3-4); that the scriptures, consequently, are an all-sufficient guide from earth to heaven.

The second view is that each child of God is led in some direct way by the Spirit in understanding God's will. People are often heard to say, "God is leading me into this understanding," or "in this way," and in saying this they mean that He is leading them through some direct guidance. While they do not disregard the scriptures altogether, they feel that they are led in some additional way into an understanding of God's will, applying John 14.26 and John 16.13 to every "believer."

This writer confesses to holding the first view and would ask those who hold to the second view the following questions:

(1) If, indeed, all believers are led directly into an understanding of God's will, why was it necessary for the first converts to continue "steadfastly in the apostles' doctrine" (Acts 2.42)? Would they not have had the same understanding of God's will as the apostles had?

(2) How do we explain the differences in doctrine and practice that exists among those who claim to be led into their understanding directly by the Lord? Differences abound among those who claim direct guidance, while the scriptures teach only "one faith" (Eph 4.4-6). Is the Lord really leading all these people into conflicting ideas? Is He the author of confusion (1 Cor 14.33)?

(3) If you could accurately communicate to me—either orally or in writing—this understanding into which you have been led, could I place as much confidence in it as I do in the writings of Matthew, Mark, Luke, John, Paul, etc.? Could I continue steadfastly in your teaching as the early Christians did in the apostles' teaching? If so, how would I know to continue steadfastly in your teaching rather than in the teaching of some person whose understanding conflicts with yours? With all these conflicts, would we not have to go back to the Bible to know what was right? And wouldn't that, in reality, take us to the first view stated in this article, which I already accept.

The truth is—the scriptures are God's divine truth (John 17.17). One can read and understand them (Eph 3.3-4). They are all-sufficient as a guide from earth to heaven (2 Tim 3.16-17). They will provide the basis for our judgment in the last day (John 12.48). Read them carefully and obey them in love.

You Wouldn't Trade?

"I wouldn't trade the feeling I have right here in my heart for all the Bibles you could stack in this building." These are the words a man once used to describe his own personal assurance of salvation—assurance based upon the wonderful feeling he had in his heart.

This writer meanwhile accepts just the opposite viewpoint. He leans on the Bible as his **sole** assurance of salvation. In fact, he wouldn't trade the assurance he finds in his Bible for the most wonderful feeling anyone ever had—nor for the **combined** testimony of feelings, preachers, parents, and even the angels of heaven.

You see, the Bible contains the promises of God, and nothing is surer than God's promises. God is the One who cannot lie (Heb 6.18). Further, whatever He promises He is able to perform (Rom 4.21). Both God's word and God's power are therefore absolutely dependable. When God promises through His Son, "He who believes and is baptized will be saved" (Mark 16.16), that promise cannot fail.

Feelings? Feelings on the other hand can deceive. Saul of Tarsus is a perfect example of one who was so deceived, for he felt that he was doing God a service when he was persecuting Christians (John 16.2; Acts 26.9-11). There must have been a time when he had a wonderful feeling in his heart, knowing that he was advancing in what he believed to be right far more rapidly than his contemporaries (Gal 1.14).

The lost people of Matthew 7.22 serve as another example of deceptive feelings, for they felt that all was well because they had prophesied in the Lord's name, and cast out devils, and done many wonderful works. Their feelings, **though backed by signs**, proved to be deceptive feelings nonetheless.

Preachers? The testimony of preachers is also inadequate assurance of salvation, for there are true teachers and there are false teachers. Jesus warned, "Beware of false prophets, who come to you in sheep's clothing, but inwardly they are ravenous wolves" (Matt 7.15). One cannot distinguish between the true and the false on the basis of pious prayers, nice personality, caring disposition, or scripture quoting ability, for any of these **could** be the sheep's clothing of which Jesus spoke. One can distinguish between them only by the teaching of the Bible; but this brings us back to that true basis of assurance spoken of earlier in this article.

Angels? The assurance of the Bible is even greater than the word of angels. "But even if we, or an angel from heaven, preach any other gospel to you than what we have preached to you, let him be accursed" (Gal 1.8).

The Bible is the word of God. Its commands are to be obeyed; its promises to be believed; its assurance to be accepted. It is the standard. All other standards will fail.

Restoration Principles in John's Epistles

Changes inevitably occur with the passing of time. New teachers arise, introducing doctrines that are false, but attractive. Each new generation tends to be more sophisticated than the former, rejecting the "outmoded" practices of their forefathers and adopting new ideas and practices.

This is not a new phenomenon. Changes occurred in the first century as they do in the twentieth. As there are "brotherhood issues" today, there were "brotherhood issues" that affected the Christians of the first century: the question of circumcision, and toward the end of the first century, Gnosticism, with its varying doctrines and corrupting morals. By the time John wrote his epistles, many changes had occurred since Pentecost in the thinking, morals, and attitudes of the people. As John addresses the changes that had occurred, he lays down three principles that should guide us in dealing with the changes of our day.

1. **When changes occur, we must go back to "the beginning," not to what has been traditionally accepted**. "Back to the beginning" is the very essence of restoration, and it is to the beginning that John leads his readers. We read from his pen, "Brethren, I write no new commandment to you, but an old commandment which you have had from the beginning" (1 John 2.7); again, "For this is the message that you heard from the beginning" (1 John 3.11; see also 2 John 5-6). John further assures his readers that "if what you heard from the beginning abides in you, you also will abide in the Son and in the Father" (1 John 2.24). Acceptance of that which is from the beginning is therefore essential to acceptance with God.

2. **When changes occur, we must go back to the source of truth, not to highly trained "clergymen" or "know-it-all" dictators in the church**. In fact, John's writings would erase all "clergy-laity" distinctions. He does not write to a few seminary-trained scholars who,

in turn, are to interpret his writings for the untrained laymen. He addresses "little children," "fathers," and "young men" (1 John 2.12-14). MacKnight, in his comments on these verses, uses the terms "new converts," "old Christians," and "vigorous Christians." All are to read John's letter, understand it, and follow its teaching. People will never return to truth as long as they allow a few learned men to do all their studying and thinking for them.

John teaches his readers to "test the spirits, whether they are of God" (1 John 4.1), rather than to follow blindly their teaching. The elect lady must determine whether or not a teacher "abides in the doctrine of Christ" before extending to him hospitality and fellowship (2 John 9-11). Gaius must not give in to the dictates of the domineering Diotrophes (3 John 9-11). John's message in all these passages is that every Christian must read, think, come to sound conclusions, and stand, even when his stand brings him into conflict with the elite of the church. This is the only way to find truth when changes occur.

3. **When changes occur, we must go back to the apostles, not to high-sounding philosophies that may be gaining popularity all around us.** The philosophies of Gnosticism were impressive. Those who espoused them took on an air of superiority. But John says of the apostles: "We are of God. He who knows God hears us; he who is not of God does not hear us. By this we know the spirit of truth and the spirit of error" (1 John 4.6). "Back to the apostles," John is saying. This is the means by which the spirits are to be tried, and false prophets are to be separated from the true. In commending Demetrius, John further says, "You know that our testimony is true" (3 John 12). We go "back to the apostles" today when we go to the New Testament scriptures. This is our only means of knowing "the spirit of truth and the spirit of error" and of standing on testimony that "is true."

We may differ in our estimation of the "restoration movement" of the nineteenth century and of its leaders, but we must not veer from the principle of restoration. There is only one answer for the religious division and corrupting doctrines of our day, and that answer is the same as it was in John's day: back to the beginning—back to the source of truth—back to the apostles. Here we take our stand! Here we withstand all enemies of truth and right! Here we know that we indeed are of God!

It's Original

"It's original," you say. Oh yeah? It may be no more original than an article I wrote recently for *Perspectives*. I thought it was original, but then ran across a similar article by Ralph Williams that had been written long before my article, which had no doubt influenced my thinking and had become such a part of me that I was sure that those thoughts were mine. My original thoughts!

Or it may be no more original than some of those original (?) thoughts that Sewell and I come up with for sermons, only to learn that our dad has presented those thoughts in sermons since we were boys. In fact, I'm wondering now who has written an article on the subject of "It's Original."

We are blessed with a rich heritage. We have heard great men preach great sermons, bringing out just about every thought imaginable from the greatest book that has ever been written. Most of the sermons we have forgotten. Nor are we able to relate specific thoughts to the men whom we first heard preach them. But those thoughts became a part of us, and those sermons, little by little, changed our lives and our thinking to bring us to our present convictions and status before God. We are indebted to so many, but especially to God, from whom all truth originates (John 17.17).

But a warning is in order at this point. For, whereas we are grateful for the truths that have been taught through the years, we must never accept any teaching as truth just because brethren have "always" believed and taught it. Humility would demand that we be slow to reject such, but truth is determined only by an examination of Bible teaching. "Your word is truth" (John 17.17). "If anyone speaks, let him speak as the oracles of God" (1 Pet 4.11). The old, accepted teaching must be examined, not only by each generation, but by every individual within that generation, with the same care with which any new teaching is examined.

Independence of thought does not demand a rejection of old, accepted teaching, but it does demand a careful examination of that teaching in the light of the scriptures.

The Power of Simplicity

Jesus Christ had a deep appreciation for simple things. His **teaching** was profound, but always simple. He reached the hearts of His hearers, not with high-sounding philosophical jargon, but with illustrations and "to the point" teaching. He could see in a farmer sowing his seed, or a lily showing forth its beauty, or a shepherd leaving his flock to seek one lost sheep, or a loving father welcoming a wayward son, a lesson that could teach some spiritual truth.

His **apostles** were chosen from the humble class. He could appreciate people, not for what they possessed, but for what they were; and, in some cases, not for what they were, but for what they could become. He recognized true quality, and true quality is often found in the simple and humble.

The **worship** He ordained was simple in nature. "Now on the first day of the week, when the disciples came together to break bread, Paul…spoke to them…" (Acts 20.7). Even the poorest could worship, for all that was required of a material nature was a little bread and fruit of the vine. Those of little talent could worship, for God was listening in view of the heart rather than the beauty of the voice.

He authorized a simple **organization** for His church, with each congregation appointing its own bishops and deacons (Phil 1.1). There were no denominational associations, conferences, or synods. There were no inter-church organizations or societies. Yet, through the simple organization given the church by the Lord, the world of the first century was thoroughly evangelized and the needy among them provided for. The Lord knew that success in His work would not be brought about through complexity of organization, but through dedication, faith, and commitment on the part of His followers. We make a terrible mistake when we try to substitute the former for the latter.

Why this simplicity? "That no flesh should glory in His presence" (1 Cor 1.29). The complex systems which men devise tend to bring glory to themselves rather than to God.

To return to the simplicity which our Lord ordained might not be impressive to the worldly-minded, but, then, Jesus Himself is not very impressive to the worldly-minded. Besides, our purpose is not to impress the worldly-minded, but to please God and bow in submission to His will. Let us do away with our super projects and complex systems. Let us learn to appreciate simple teaching and simple ways. Above all, let us learn to appreciate **Bible** teaching and **Bible** ways.

We like the following quote from Ed Harrell: "How foolish we are to think that God will be impressed with our voices when we sing; after all, He hears the angels sing! How foolish to think He will be impressed with our cathedrals; remember, He made the Grand Canyon!" What He is seeking for is a heart that is pure, loving, and obedient to His will. And that's simple.

God-Consciousness

A truly godly man is one who lives with a constant realization of God's divine presence. He is God-conscious. When he awakes in the morning, there is God. As he dresses for work, there is God. As he goes in to breakfast with his family, as he drives to work, as he works through the day, as he drives home, as he spends the evening hours, as he lies down on his bed at the close of the day, there is God.

Enoch was a man who was God-conscious, for he "walked with God" (Gen 5.24). He enjoyed constant companionship with God. Wherever Enoch went, God went with him, and Enoch was always aware that He was there. He could not flee from God's presence (Psa 139.7), nor did he seek to do so. He was a godly man.

How fortunate is that man who has developed within himself this God-consciousness. It is easy for him to pray, for God is to him a close, ever near, companion whose "ears are open to [his] prayers" (1 Pet 3.12). His talking with God is as natural as his talking with any companion.

He does not fear, for he just places his hand in God's in his times of trouble. "God is our refuge and strength, a very present help in trouble. Therefore we will not fear..." (Psa 46.1-2). Even when walking "through the valley of the shadow of death," he can "fear no evil," for God is with him.

The power of temptation is greatly reduced, for he never forgets that "all things are naked and open to the eyes of Him to whom we must give account" (Heb 4.13). His desire to please his ever-present God is greater than the power of temptation.

He is thankful, recognizing God, with whom he walks, to be the source of "every good gift and every perfect gift" (Jas 1.17).

He loves God. He talks to God. He walks with God. He is always conscious of God's presence. He is never without God. Yet, this relationship never degenerates into a "buddy-buddy" relationship, for he reverences God; he recognizes His awesomeness; he gratefully acknowledges his own personal unworthiness of such a relationship with Almighty God.

This is the very essence of godliness. Someone years ago, observing the similarity between "godliness" and "God-like-ness," assumed that the two words meant the same. That false assumption was passed to others, and has now gained a strong foothold in the thinking of a great number of people. W.E. Vine says that godliness "denotes that piety which, characterized by a god-ward attitude, does that which is well pleasing to Him." A godly person, then, is one who has a god-ward attitude, and whose constant consciousness of God leads him to be obedient to Him.

While visiting in a hospital, recently, we observed this sign, "Have you said 'Thank you, God' today?" A godly person probably would have done so. Have **you** said, "thank you, God" today?

My Prayer

Lord, help me never to become callous of heart. Help me to be sensitive to the pains and hurts of others.

Let me feel a genuine thrill on truly thrilling occasions: when two young Christians are joined in marriage; when some young man preaches his first gospel sermon, or when some new convert leads his first prayer; when a newborn baby cries, or when some elderly person successfully passes one more milestone in his life; when a sinner responds to be baptized, or when a brother returns.

Lord, I do not want to shut out from my own life the sorrows of others. Make me to weep when tears are in order: when a doctor has just given a frightening report; when parents grieve over their delinquent child; when tears flow from the eyes of a motherless child, or of a childless mother; when a struggling brother or sister has slipped back into sin; when a man has just been forsaken by the wife of his youth; when all hope seems gone among those who had hoped.

Help me to be excited over the successes of others: when someone achieves something that I've never been able to achieve; when some worthy man is appointed an elder of the church; when someone's son is graduated with honors; when some couple moves into that long awaited new home; when some young man's preaching ability has obviously surpassed mine. Above all, Lord, don't let me be jealous.

Lord, help me to be like Thee: compassionate, kind, merciful, gracious, slow to anger, plenteous in mercy, touched with the feeling of others' infirmities, able to weep, ready to rejoice, emotional, and loving. Let me deny self, and esteem others better than myself.

And, Lord, let me never become hardened to sin. Help me to hate sin, to weep blinding tears over my own sins, to maintain a conscience void of offense. May I be repulsed and grieved over the sins of others.

Lord, help me never to become callous of heart, for should I do so, I could no longer render effective service to Thee or to my fellowman, and I would forfeit all hope of real happiness, both in this life and in that which is to come.

Before God—Before Men

"Take heed that you do not do your charitable deeds before men, to be seen by them. Otherwise you have no reward from your Father in heaven" (Matt 6.1).

True righteousness is primarily "God-conscious" rather than "man-conscious." God is pleased as we sing His praises, or teach His truth, or lead in prayer, or help the needy, or give to support His work, if our purpose is to gain His approval and bring glory to His name. Woe to that person who sings for the purpose of displaying his beautiful voice. Woe to that person who seeks the praise of men as he leads in prayer. Woe to that preacher who "tickles the ears" of his listeners. Woe to that person who gives to be seen of men. When he gains their praises, he "has his reward in full;" none awaits him from the Father in heaven.

In keeping with this teaching, the Bible reveals God's judgment of two different couples, one enjoying God's approval, the other suffering His disapproval.

God disapproved of Ananias and Sapphira (Acts 5.1-11). His disapproval was not because of the amount of their offering. They had brought a very liberal offering. They had even sold a possession in order to give, and while we do not know what portion they brought, they obviously brought what they thought would be sufficient to impress the apostles. But herein lies the key to their real problem: They were more conscious of **men's** reaction to their benevolence than they were of **God's**. Had they been conscious of God in what they did, and had they been seeking His approval, they would not have lied. But they did their righteousness "**before men**, to be seen by them," and in their concern for impressing men, they lied concerning the amount which they brought.

In contrast to Ananias and Sapphira, there were Zacharias and Elizabeth of whom it was said, "And they were both righteous **before God**" (Luke 1.6). While many no doubt observed their righteousness, and as a result glorified the Father in heaven (Matt 5.16), Zacharias and Elizabeth obviously were not as concerned for man's approval as they were for God's approval. It was God's approval that they sought; it was His approval that they gained.

God blessed Zacharias and Elizabeth, choosing them to be the parents of John, the forerunner of Christ. He punished Ananias and Sapphira with immediate death, and, in keeping with Jesus' statement of Matthew 6.1, they "have no reward from your Father who is in heaven."

Hypocrisy is loathsome to the Lord. For a person to appear outwardly religious and sincere while inwardly he only desires the praise and approval of men is to be guilty of gross hypocrisy. Let us seek always to do our righteousness before God to be seen of Him. The glorious and eternal "reward of the Father" cannot be compared with the fickle and fleeting praise of men.

Not Our—But His Workmanship

"For we are His workmanship, created in Christ Jesus for good works, which God prepared beforehand that we should walk in them" (Eph 2.10).

When one is baptized he becomes a new creation, but he is not the creation of any man. He is the workmanship of God.

He is not the workmanship of the person who converted him—not primarily, anyway. Man can teach, influence, persuade, and baptize; but only God can cleanse, forgive, raise a person to sit with Christ in the heavenly places, and give him life. He is God's creation—God's workmanship. Just as surely as no man could create an "Adam," just that surely can no man create a new creature in Christ.

Neither is one self-made. In Christ, one does not lift himself "by his own bootstraps." Christianity is not a "do-it-yourself" religion—not in the fullest sense. One does not effect his own salvation through his own merit. Rather, in obedience to the gospel and faithfulness as a Christian, he places himself as clay in God's hand, to become the work of the divine Potter, who molds, shapes, and perfects him that he might be fashioned in the image of His Son.

He is the workmanship of God because his salvation is "by grace...through faith...the gift of God" (Eph 2.8-9).

If one's salvation were of meritorious works, he would not be the workmanship of God. This is the primary thrust of the passage.

The workmanship of God exists as a monument to the greatness of a potter; as a beautiful painting is a monument to an artist, so a mature and perfected Christian is a monument to the marvelous power of God. Such a person is a product of God's grace and exists for "the praise of His glory" (Eph 1.6,12,14; 3.14-19). That God could take a Peter, a John, a Saul of Tarsus, an Aquila, a Priscilla, a John Mark, and mold him or her into the lovely vessel each became is a manifestation of His greatness. That He could do the same for people this writer has known and observed equally manifests His greatness. That He can and will do the same for me if I will but submit myself to His care in humble obedience, trust, and prayer is the greatest marvel of all. "I am so glad that Jesus loves me...Jesus loves even me" (P.P. Bliss).

The workmanship of God must be handled with care. Such a person is special, precious, and priceless to God. As one is cautious in handling a family heirloom or rare piece of pottery fashioned by the hands of a master, so he must be cautious in his handling of that creation, which is the work of God. "Do not destroy the work of God for the sake of food," Paul warned the Romans (Rom 14.20).

That person toward whose tender conscience you are showing little regard or whose soul you are placing in jeopardy is the work of God. Love that person. Appreciate him. Be tender toward him. Recognize his value. Handle with care!

The workmanship of God must never be content until it is brought to perfection. "Finish then thy new creation," Charles Wesley wrote in his familiar hymn, "Love Divine." In keeping with this, Paul could express his confidence in the Philippian Christians, "That He who has begun a good work in you will complete it until the day of Jesus Christ" (Phil 1.6-7). Only those who remain in the Potter's hands until brought to completion and perfection become vessels of honor. All others become marred and fit only for destruction (2 Tim 2.19-21).

Let no man, then, boast of himself. Self-righteousness has no place in the heart of a Christian. If any man boast, "let him glory in the LORD" (1 Cor 1.31) and "in the cross of our Lord Jesus Christ" (Gal 6.14). We are His workmanship.

Not Our—But His Might

"Finally, my brethren, be strong in the Lord and in the power of His might" (Eph 6.10).

In our battle against Satan, we cannot be victorious on the basis of our own strength. We must rely on the strength and might of the Lord.

> Did we in our own strength confide
> Our striving would be losing;
> Were not the right One on our side
> The Man of God's own choosing.
> Dost ask who that may be?
> Christ Jesus, it is He,
> Lord Sabaoth is His name,
> From age to age the same,
> And He must win the battle.
>
> *–Martin Luther*

The reason we cannot win on the basis of our own strength is because of the nature of the foe. "We do not wrestle against flesh and blood" (Eph 6.12). If it were our own strength against another man's strength, we might be victorious on our own. The foe, however, is a spiritual foe and a spiritual foe can be overcome only through the power of God's might.

How to Rely on the Lord's Might

1. **Through taking on the armor** which He supplies: salvation as our helmet, righteousness as our breastplate, truth as our girdle, the preparation of the gospel of peace as our footwear, faith as our shield, and the word of God as our sword. There are those who rely on human philosophy, positive thinking, transcendental meditation, monasticism, self-deprivation, etc., for their armor. All such "arms of flesh" will fail.

2. **Through constant prayer to the Lord for help**. "Praying always with all prayer and supplication in the Spirit…" (Eph 6.18). The Lord helps us in so many ways. He shields us from temptation (Matt 6.13). He tempers temptation when it does come (1 Cor 10.13). He brings good influences into our lives (Rom 1.12). He forgives when we are overcome (1 John 1.7, 9). But He does not want us taking Him for granted. We must ask the Lord for help and thank Him as He brings us safely through each battle.

3. **Through full expectation of victory**. Let no one enter this battle with a defeatist attitude. Victory is assured for all who will rely upon the strength of the Lord. The words "that ye may be able" appear three times in the Ephesians 6 passage (11,13, 16). It is as though the Lord shows us the enemy and we, impressed with the enemy's obvious strength, begin to despair; then the Lord says, "You can defeat him; here is your armor, put on every piece; stay close to me, I'll help you fight; if you suffer a knockdown, I'll pick you up; just keep fighting; persevere; watch; the victory is yours!"

Stand, Therefore

We must, stand, however, if we would win the battle. Stand! Stand! Stand! The word appears three times in the text (Eph 6.11,13,14). The best armor in the world is of little value if there is a coward inside. It is not unusual to find a man who seems to be well equipped for battle. He knows the scriptures, has studied the meaning of scripture, has memorized extensively, has all the appearance of a great soldier—but when the first challenge is issued, he breaks into a sweat, wavers, vacillates, and compromises until an observer really can't tell which side he is on. He doesn't stand. Such a person faces sure defeat. Victory is assured, but only for those who will stand.

The battle rages. The struggle is great. The enemy is formidable. The stakes are great—eternal in nature, in fact. Thank the Lord—the hope for victory rests not on ours, but upon His strength and might.

Must We See the Answer?

"How can I be sure that God is answering my prayers?" someone asks. "How can I positively pinpoint this event or that event as His final and complete answer?" We are hearing such questions rather frequently these days.

One who feels the necessity of pinpointing the answer to his prayer, and questions that his prayer is answered unless he can do so, may have a problem with his faith. He may want to walk by sight rather than by faith. Acceptable prayer is an outgrowth of complete trust in God, trust that does not have to see and identify.

An employer has an employee in whom he has complete trust and confidence. A rather complex problem arises. Considerable time, thought, and research will be required if the problem is brought to a reasonable solution. But knowing the competence of his employee and having complete trust in him as a responsible man of unquestioned loyalty and integrity, the employer calls the employee in, lays the problem before him, turns the matter over to him in its entirety, and never even asks about the outcome. Such trustworthy employees are obviously rare, but they do exist.

Our point is this. If an employer can place this kind of confidence in a trustworthy, but fallible, employee, can we not place equal—no, infinitely greater!—confidence in our infallible heavenly Father? Can we not learn to place our problems and burdens on Him, and know that He will bring them to the very best possible solution according to His will? And can we not come to believe that He will do so without our having to see, pinpoint, and interpret the outcome for ourselves? Is it not even possible that the full outcome will not be felt until far into the future, long after we are gone from this burden-filled world? "Casting all your care upon Him, for He cares for you" (1 Pet 5.7; see also 1 John 5.14-15).

The words "best possible solution" are key words at this point, however. Our faith must not be just in the fact that God will act, but that He will act so as to bring about the best possible solution, even if that solution proves to be contrary to what we would desire or seek. We must be willing to turn our problems over to God for His disposition, and then to say in full submission to His will, "It is the LORD. Let Him do what seems good to Him" (1 Sam 3.18). Jesus manifested this kind of trust and submission (Matt 26.39-44). So did the great characters of the Old Testament (Heb 11). So did the apostles (2 Cor 4.13-14). And so must we.

Wonderfully blessed is the person who has this kind of faith. While others fret and worry, he lets his anxieties and requests "be made known to God" (Phil 4.6). While others are filled with turmoil and fear, he possesses "the peace of God, which surpasses all understanding…." "But let him ask in faith, with no doubting…" (Jas 1.6).

On a Daily Basis

A man, asked recently to describe memories of his college days of twenty-five years ago, replied, "A few big moments; many goofs; but, overall, pleasant memories."

Would these words not describe our memories of life generally? As we recall our years, there are always the "big" moments, the emotional "highs," that we love to relish. Then there are the "goofs," the embarrassing occasions that just keep coming back to haunt us. But through it all the pleasant memories sufficiently prevail to enable us to feel generally good about life.

But, in reality, success or failure in life is not determined by the "big moments" or "the goofs." We will not be eternally saved on the basis of a few great spiritual achievements or eternally lost on the basis of a few gross mistakes (assuming they have been repented of). Life consists of everyday actions and decisions, and it is these that bring ultimate success or failure, eternal happiness or eternal damnation. "If anyone desires to come after Me, let him deny himself, and take up his cross daily, and follow Me" (Luke 9.23).

It is one thing to express concern for our children as we talk of their future spirituality and faithfulness. It is quite another thing to provide on a daily basis a spiritual atmosphere in the home, a good example of godliness and faithfulness, consistent and loving discipline, and a love for God and respect for fellow man that are so essential to the training of our children. It's the little impressions that are made day by day that prove to be so decisive.

It is one thing to dream of some day being appointed an elder in the church. It is quite another thing to put forth the effort on a daily basis to learn the scriptures, to develop leadership ability, to grow spiritually, and to live so as to gain the confidence of a discerning congregation. One does not qualify for the eldership in one big leap. It comes through daily development.

It is one thing to talk a "good line" on priorities. It is quite another thing to put God first on a daily basis. The devil knows so many ways to test our resolve in these realms. Our intentions are good, but through his subtlety he has us selling our souls for a mess of pottage or thirty pieces of silver.

It is one thing to think that we would **die** for the Lord if our faith were so tested. It is quite another thing truly to live for Him on a daily basis. Egos may be fed on the "big moments," but true spirituality develops through daily prayer, study, and meditation.

Our lesson is this. Set your goals for the future, and set them high. But recognize that it's the little, day-by-day moments, the often forgotten moments, accumulating through the years that truly shape our destiny. Tomorrow's success depends upon the choices and decisions that are made today. Make them with care.

Self-Control

What is the value of self-control? Self-control is that which enables us to hold our tongues when we are tempted to viciously put someone in his place once and for all…or when we know a juicy bit of gossip that would be entertaining to the group and would turn us into the "life of the party"…or when an occasion almost demands that we betray a confidence that must not be betrayed under any circumstances.

Self-control is that which enables us to control our passions when another is provoking us to anger…that keeps the clinched fists in the pockets when the agitator is only half our size…that keeps the lips sealed when another is railing and swearing at us. Self-control is that which enables us to be like our Lord "who, when He was reviled, did not revile in return; when He suffered, He did not threaten, but committed Himself to Him who judges righteously" (1 Pet 2.23).

Self-control is that which enables us to maintain purity of heart and to thrust out evil thoughts before they can take root…that enables us to place the best possible construction on another person's actions when unproven rumors could easily destroy our confidence in him…that helps us to maintain a cheerful disposition when everything around us has turned sour. Self-control is that which enables us to bring "every thought into captivity to the obedience of Christ" (2 Cor 10.5). Self-control is that which enables us to love the unlovable and to hate that which the world loves.

Self-control is that which enables us to rule our appetites...to say "no" when our lusts would lead us to sin or when that which is harmful to our health is placed before us. Self-control is that which enables the smoker to put down his cigarettes and the alcoholic to put down his drink and never return to it. Self-control is that which enables us to rule rather than to be enslaved.

The Bible does not glorify the indifferent and impassive. It is not our goal to be uncaring. To be like Paul we must be able to have our spirits stirred within us when we are surrounded by evil (Acts 17.16). To be like our Lord we must sometimes feel anger when surrounded by hypocritical self-righteousness (Mark 3.5); we must even react with outbursts of goodness on occasions, as when the Lord cleansed the temple (John 2.13-17). But all such outbursts must be tempered with self-control, that in our anger we "do not sin" (Eph 4.26).

God does not view our uncontrolled actions with amusement. Our temper tantrums and harsh, unbridled words are soul threatening, a potential bar to the abundant entrance into the Lord's everlasting kingdom (2 Pet 1.5-11). We must not minimize the danger. We must not surrender to this evil.

What is the value of self-control? It is one of the qualities that enable us to go to heaven. The possessor of it is rich indeed.

Outbursts of Goodness

"But the fruit of the Spirit is love, joy, peace, longsuffering, kindness, goodness..." (Gal 5.22). In defining "goodness" Trench suggests that the word includes the "sterner qualities by which doing good to others is not necessarily by gentle means" *(Expository Dictionary of New Testament Words,* W.E. Vine, p. 165). Two examples in the life of Christ are given to illustrate this sterner type of goodness: His cleansing of the temple (Matt 21.12-13), and His denunciation of the scribes and Pharisees (Matt 23.13-33). I suppose we could call such action "outbursts of goodness."

Trench may be right or wrong in his definition, but we are quite sure that some outbursts of goodness are needed in our day. A sudden move toward the "off" knob on our TV sets, accompanied by some well-chosen words of disapproval, might help our children to know that we hate the filth, the profanity, the lasciviousness that so often is pictured. Or is it possible that we have been exposed for so long to this evil, that we really have "gotten used to it," and are no longer repulsed by it?

We wonder how many churches might have been saved from present-day innovations through some outbursts of goodness. Spontaneous reaction from brethren who through the years have been respected for their knowledge, sincerity, levelheadedness, love, and genuineness has no doubt given pause on many occasions to those who would introduce programs for which there was no Bible authority.

The list is almost endless: false doctrine, drunkenness, prejudice, immodesty, drug use, etc. All such justify occasional outbursts of goodness.

One should be sure, however, that his outburst is one of **goodness**. Our children can see "right through" our hypocrisy. Our brethren can, too. Besides, hypocrisy is dishonest and sinful.

True goodness, then, begins within the heart. There it grows until it overflows, and sometimes its overflow will be in the form of an outburst, an outburst that is genuine and spontaneous, producing great benefits. One who truly abhors that which is evil is going to demonstrate his abhorrence, **naturally** and **effectively**. This is the "goodness" that is the "fruit of the Spirit."

No License to Sin

God's mercy must not be viewed as a license to sin. "How shall we who died to sin live any longer in it?" (Rom 6.2)

Accidents occur occasionally at the Hall house, most frequently at the dinner table. A glass of water is knocked over—a full one, of course. A pained expression comes over the face of the fumbling party. But no great fuss results. Apologies are made; the mess cleaned up; and everything returns to normal. But if one of our children were to ask, "Daddy, may I knock over a glass of water?" the answer would be "No." Mother's patience does not constitute permission to spill water. Nor will we allow carelessness at the dinner table. Words of caution are often expressed, that our children **spill not the water**; but if they, in spite of their caution, and because of human frailty, knock over the water, patience and forgiveness will be extended.

Is not this really the message of the Holy Spirit in 1 John 2.1: "My little children, these things I write to you so that you may not sin. And if anyone sins, we have an Advocate with the Father, Jesus Christ the righteous"?

God does not grant permission to commit even one sin. If a man could somehow communicate directly to God, and make his request, "Lord, I have been faithful in attendance for a long time; I haven't missed a service in twenty years; so, Lord, won't it be all right if I fail *to* break bread with Thy people just this one time so I can do what I want to do; won't you let me off just this once?" Do we really think the Lord would grant him permission? Or suppose his request was to tell just one lie, or engage in just one dishonest business deal, or to cover up just once the fact that he is a Christian? Would the Lord grant permission to sin? "These things I write to you, **so that you may not sin**."

Neither will the Lord allow carelessness. He demands that we study diligently and objectively His word and will. "These things **I write to you** so that you may not sin." Can we believe that the person who through carelessness fails to read and study that which is written unto him for the expressed purpose of keeping him from sin, or the person who is so prejudiced that he is blinded to what is written can claim God's mercy because of his ignorance? We hardly think so!

Toward whom then is God's grace extended? It is extended to those who are His children; who seek diligently for the light of His word; who continually walk in that light; who determine never to "give place to the devil;" who recognize that in spite of their efforts, however, they do sin, and consequently turn humbly and continually to God for forgiveness, confessing their sins. These are the ones who have an "Advocate with the Father, Jesus Christ the righteous" (1 John 1.5-2.1). We find joy in holding out hope and assurance to others, but beyond this teaching we dare not go.

Forgetting and Reaching

A man never reaches a point in his life when he can relax in his struggle against the evil one. No one was more aware of this fact than was the apostle Paul. While on his third preaching tour, the mature, experienced apostle wrote to the saints in Corinth: "But I discipline my body and bring it into subjection, lest, when I have preached to others, I myself should become disqualified" (1 Cor 9.27). Later, while in prison at Rome, writing to his beloved in Philippi, he acknowledged that he had not already attained, neither was already perfect; that considerable struggle yet lay ahead (Phil 3.12). Crucial in that struggle was Paul's ability to **forget** some things.

1. **Paul had to forget what might have been**. This writer once heard a young entertainer make the statement, "I'm going to give it all up; a person just cannot be a Christian and be successful in the entertainment field." All who heard the statement applauded the faith of the young man, and marveled at his strength as he went back home to carry out his resolution. But the young man could never forget what might have been. Dreams of fame and fortune kept entering his mind. Finally the lure of "what might have been" overcame him, and he returned to that life that would sift, tempt, and eventually destroy his soul.

As a young man, Paul had shown great promise of worldly fame. Few men had shown more promise. Trained at the feet of Gamaliel, he had "advanced in Judaism beyond many of [his] contemporaries" (Gal 1.14). He had given up his claim to fortune and fame, however, in order to be a Christian. "But what things were gain to me, these I have counted loss for Christ" (Phil 3.7). How easy it might have been for Paul, imprisoned in Rome, with many of his companions forsaking him, to have begun to grieve over "what might have been." Had he done so, his effectiveness as a servant of the Lord would have ended and he very likely would have lost his soul.

2. **Paul had to forget the sins of the past.** It is true that Paul never forgot that he was a sinner saved by grace. He frequently spoke of his days as a persecutor and once referred to himself as the chief of sinners (1Tim 1.15). But his sins had been forgiven, washed away by the blood of Christ (Acts 22.16). From the day he was baptized he ceased to brood over his sins and became a rejoicing Christian, trusting the assurance of God's word that his sins were all forgiven. Satan gets an advantage over the man who cannot forget the sins of the past (2 Cor 2.6-11). Paul's ability to forget, consequently, was vital to his continued faithfulness to the Lord.

3. **Paul had to forget the failures of the past.** Failures are discouraging, and the person who grieves over his failures will accomplish little in life. Paul knew failure. There was little to show for his efforts in Athens. The Galatians had followed after a perverted gospel. Many whom he had converted had fallen away. Judaizers had undermined his teaching and reputation in many cities where he had worked. Lesser men would have thrown up their hands in despair, bemoaned their mistreatment, and fallen victim to self-pity, one of the devil's most effective tools. Paul had to forget.

4. **Paul had to forget the successes of the past.** There had been many. Strong churches in Ephesus, Philippi, Thessalonica, and many other cities stood as concrete evidence of the effectiveness of Paul's work. Great men, such as Titus, Timothy, and Epaphras, had been converted by him. He could have easily said, "Look what I've done; now it's time to turn the work over to the younger men." Had he done so, he would have ceased his running before he had "finished the course," and certainly would have been lost.

Paul had to forget, and Paul could forget. Writing to the Philippians, he said, "Brethren, I do not count myself to have apprehended; but one thing I do, forgetting those things which are behind and reaching forward to those things which are ahead, I press toward the goal for the prize of the upward call of God in Christ Jesus" (Phil 3.13-14). **Forgetting and reaching forth**! Here is the key to faithful service to the Lord. Paul serves as a wonderful example. He could forget the thing he had to forget, and reach forth to greater service in the Lord's vineyard, to continued purity of life, to greater and greater accomplishments for the Lord, to the prize of the high calling of God in Christ Jesus.

A wonderful award awaits those who can forget and reach forth. Paul could say as he neared death, "Finally there is laid up for me the crown of righteousness, which the Lord, the righteous judge, will give to me on that Day." (2 Tim 4.8). And to all of us the Lord says, "Be faithful until death, and I will give you the crown of life." (Rev 2:10). We must persevere. We must not turn back.

To My Young Adult Friends

You're out of school now and have your own job and apartment. Congratulations! I well remember the joy of that new-found independence and the satisfaction that comes from "making it on your own." But your new position in life carries with it new responsibilities.

Are you giving as you ought? It's a rather big jump from the $5.00 you gave of the money Mother and Dad sent you to the $50, $60, or $70 that you ought to be giving now. And I know that you may feel that you can't afford to give that much; that those payments on your car, your rent, your clothes, your furniture, etc., pretty well consume all your income. But the Lord must come first. This is the meaning of Matthew 6.33: "But seek first the kingdom of God and His righteousness, and all these things will be added to you." Consider also God's appeal (and promise) to the Jews in Malachi 3.8-10. You might have to settle for a less attractive apartment or car, or do without that stereo or new outfit that you want so badly. But don't fail to give as you ought. Above all, be sure you don't spend more on fun and recreation than you give in the Lord's service.

Are you accepting your responsibilities toward the sick and the bereaved? Yes, I know that has seemed to be the responsibility of Mother and Dad and other older people up to this time; and I know, too, that you are busy with your job and that you enjoy doing "fun" things with others of your age, but God gives to all these responsibilities (Matt 25.31-46). You can surely take a few hours each week to make a visit or two and to send cards to the sick. And don't forget the elderly. They receive a special boost when young people genuinely enjoy being with them. Maybe there's room in your heart for a few extra "grandparents." It is possible, too, that their friendship could fill a void in your own life. I hear a lot of young people talking about "finding themselves." I hope you will be more concerned with "losing yourself" in favor of God and others.

Guard your morals diligently. Mother and Dad are no longer there to say "No." You must now evaluate the teaching you have received and determine whether to follow it or assume a compromising position with the world. Dare to be a Daniel! Resist the pressures! Keep yourself as clean and beautiful on the inside as you long to be on the outside. The devil does not necessarily seek a total rebellion at this point, for he knows that compromise will bring you eventually into his grasp.

I want you to know that I'm pulling for you. Many of you are special to me, and you are a great encouragement to me. Your presence at gospel meetings thrills me. Be true to yourself—now and always, and, above all, never, never let God down. Happiness in life or misery in life depends so greatly on the decisions made in youth. Your own personal maturity will be the determining factor.

The 'Marked Door" Philosophy

We have all heard of "Christian" colleges, "Christian" camps, "Christian" bookstores, etc. But have you heard of "Christian" doors? A Christian door is one so carved as to suggest a cross on the upper half and an open Bible on the lower half. Such doors are manufactured in our country and are bought by religious people as symbols of piety.

The Christian door did not originate, however, as a symbol of piety primarily, but as a hospitable message to the weary traveler looking for a safe place to stay. Neither was it a mass-produced factory item to the 18th or 19th-century owner, but was a door laboriously chiseled and carved, placed at the front of the house, carrying a silent, but powerful, message to the passerby, "Christians live here; you can stop for the night in peace and safety. Welcome!"

We are impressed! Here were people who were not just reluctantly willing to extend hospitality, but went to great effort to mark their doors as an enticement to the tired traveler to stop at their house for his needed rest. We are reminded of the Shunammite couple who built a little chamber onto their house, and furnished it with a bed, a table, a stool, and a candlestick, so that whenever Elisha passed through their country, he would have a comfortable place to stay (2 Kgs 4.8-10), and it would be at their house. "Hospitality without grumbling" the Bible calls it (1 Pet 4.9).

We are not advocating the purchase of Christian doors as symbols of piety, but we are advocating the "marked door" philosophy that views hospitality as a cherished privilege rather than a despised necessity. We appreciate those who can get excited over someone's being at their house. Most business meeting arguments are repulsive, but there is something refreshing about a dispute over "who's going to keep the preacher?" when such disputes arise, not through selfish ambition and vainglory, but through a genuine love on the part of people for having the preacher at their house.

The development of a "marked door" philosophy can transform a dead church into an active, working congregation. When people start adding a few extra potatoes to the Sunday dinner so they can invite visitors to their house, when people open their homes for Bible study groups, when people welcome newcomers with a "get acquainted" party, when people just like to have good folks over, when the homes of a congregation generally become rejoicing places for those who rejoice or havens of sympathy for those who weep, the effects will be dramatic and the fruits eternal.

The "marked door" philosophy works only among the unselfish. We "chisel out our doors" by turning off the TV, putting down the newspaper, going to a little extra trouble, and even putting up with an occasional old grouch who appreciates nothing and specializes in making everybody miserable. But in the long run those who develop it are richly blessed, both now and in eternity.

The Phone Call that was Never Made

It's Sunday afternoon, and you and your family are invited to the Smiths for sandwiches and dessert after the evening service. The invitation was extended earlier in the week and you accepted. But now something else has come up that you would rather do, so you go to the phone to cancel your engagement. But before you dial, think for a moment....

At the very time you are thinking of canceling, others are having similar thoughts. Within one hour, Mrs. Smith will receive calls from five of the seven couples she has invited, saying that, they won't be coming. It's too late to invite others. It's too late to cancel plans altogether. Food will be wasted; time will have been wasted; the occasion will not be as happy and relaxed because of the smaller number; and Mrs. Smith will be hurt and deeply disappointed. **If you call, your cancellation will be unfair to Mrs. Smith**.

Were you cancelling because of an emergency, your cancellation would be legitimate. But that's not why you are canceling. You are canceling because there is something *you* would rather do. You are only thinking of self rather than of others. You were prepared to enjoy the Smiths' hospitality unless something that sounded more exciting and enjoyable was to come up. **If you call, your cancellation will demonstrate your selfishness and lack of regard for the Smiths**.

Mrs. Smith will be so discouraged by the cancellations that she will find it hard to invite another group in. She knows that the Bible says, "Be hospitable to one another without grumbling" (1 Pet 4.9). And that God's people are to be "hospitable" (Tit 1.8). In fact, this is why she had included you in the group she was inviting. She wanted to become better acquainted with you, to build a friendship with you, and to help you to form close ties with others in the church. But it will all fall through. The only ones that will end up coming will be their closest friends. The primary purpose in extending hospitality will be thwarted. It will be hard to try again. **If you call, your cancellation will prove to be a discouragement to Mrs. Smith in doing God's will**.

Mrs. Smith will, in time, throw off her discouragement and invite another group in, but, right or wrong, you probably will not be included. She will be inviting those whom she is quite sure will appreciate the invitation and will not let her down. You will find yourself criticizing Mrs. Smith for inviting "the same old ones all the time," but those "same old ones" are the people who accept invitations, keep their appointments, and truly enjoy their time in the homes of others. You will soon observe that these "same old ones" are the ones everybody invites, for they obviously like to be with people. Meanwhile, you will find yourself more and more isolated from Christians. **If you call, your cancellation, in time, will find you spending less time with God's people and becoming more negative toward them**.

In canceling, you are not being kind; you are acting unbecomingly toward Mrs. Smith; you are seeking your own interests rather than the interests of others. **If you call, your cancellation will demonstrate a lack of love for others** (1 Cor 13.4-8).

So, before you pick up that phone, think about others, and you might just go on to the Smiths after all. In fact, you might just go through a complete attitude change, developing a positive feeling toward the evening. Having changed your attitude, you will enjoy the time with other Christians. You will see that Mrs. Smith is really glad that you came. You might even want to have the same group over to your house sometime, and you will be hoping---oh how strongly you will hope!—that none of them will call to cancel. You will become a better person, more loving, more hospitable, and more involved with other Christians, all because of the phone call that was never made.

Five Minutes and Ten Cents

Recently, while passing through a town on my way to a meeting, I remembered a lady whose mother had recently experienced a very serious illness. Concerned, I pulled off the freeway, found a nearby phone booth, and called the lady. It took only five minutes and ten cents, but as I drove back onto that freeway, I felt real warmth in my heart—a warmth that money cannot buy—knowing that I had expressed in a small way my concern for another.

But as I traveled on down that freeway, I could not help but wonder how many times I had faced a similar situation when five minutes and ten cents could have accomplished great good, only to keep moving along my own selfish way, not pausing to help my fellowman. We tend to regard too lightly the small, everyday gestures that can be so meaningful. Jesus once said, "And whoever gives one of these little ones only a cup of cold water in the name of a disciple, assuredly, I say to you, he shall by no means lose his reward" (Matt 10.42).

Mary, the sister of Martha and Lazarus, once anointed Jesus with an ointment—a small deed really—but wherever the gospel is preached, this incident is told for a memorial of her (Matt 26.13).

But let me give credit to the good lady mentioned above. She seemed to appreciate my little gesture so much. So often people are ungrateful and take for granted the little things done for them. They take away the joy of doing the little thoughtful deeds by their ungrateful attitude. But not this lady. Her show of appreciation contributed greatly to that warmth in my heart. I stopped to help her, but she in turn helped me; in fact, she made my day.

Let us remember to be thoughtful of others. That get well card, that telephone call, that short visit, that word of commendation, that expression of concern, may provide lasting cheer to someone in need. And it won't take long or cost much money. Too, let us remember to accept the little kindnesses of others graciously, with genuine appreciation. For these are the little things that bring sunshine into our lives and help us to prepare for eternity.

Mark These People

Quickly now—what type of people are to be marked by Christians according to the scriptures? Those who cause divisions and offenses contrary to Christ's doctrine? Yes, for so we are taught in Romans 16.17.

There is another type of person to be marked, however. "Brethren, be followers together of me, and mark them which walk so as ye have us for an ensample" (Phil 3.17 KJV). The word "mark" is not synonymous with the word "withdraw." According to W.E. Vine the word means "to look at, behold, watch, and contemplate." Those who are evil, then, are to be **marked** and **avoided**; while those who walk in God's way are to be **marked** and **followed**.

Godly elders should be marked. Elders are to be examples to the flock (I Pet 5.3). They are to be men whose character is above reproach, who rule their own house well, who are hospitable, and whose sound teaching can convict the gainsayers. We know such elders, and their example is priceless. Even after such men have passed on, they are to be remembered: "Remember those who rule over you, who have spoken the word of God to you, whose faith follow (a similar word to mark-BH), considering the outcome of their conduct" (Heb 13.7). Thank God for godly elders; mark them and follow their good example!

Godly women should be marked. If there are women in the congregation who stand out for their piety and humility, whose major attractiveness is their "meek and quiet spirit," who have adorned themselves with good works, who love their husband and children, who find joy and contentment in being a wife and mother and keeper at home, who feel no resentment toward their position of subjection to man, who have devoted their lives to doing God's will—**and there are such women in every congregation**—then mark these godly women and follow their example. In these days when the women's liberation movement is affecting so many and actually intimidating many women who want to do right, it is wonderful to have godly women in the church who are able to lead the way and provide a role model for other women who are Christians. Thank God for godly women; mark them and follow their good example!

Godly preachers should be marked. Not all preachers are godly, but most of the gospel preachers of our acquaintance are godly men whose lives speak as effectively as do their lips. They do their work, not as hirelings, but as men concerned for truth and the souls of men and women. Mark such men and follow their example!

Godly parents, godly young people, godly older people, godly suffering people, godly dying people—the godly faithful! How sad that some are so blinded by the faults of the few that they cannot see the virtues of the many.

Good people are all around us. Let's look for them, contemplate their good qualities, mark them, and follow their example.

Honor Our Enemies?

One of the strangest inconsistencies that exist among God's people is their tendency to honor their greatest enemies. Consider the Christians of James' day. They were so flattered when rich men entered their assemblies that they would pompously say to them, "Sit here in a good place," forgetting that they represented the very type who had oppressed them, drawn them before the judgment seats, and blasphemed that worthy name by which they were called (Jas 2.1-7). They were "looking up" to the enemies of truth and righteousness while "looking down" on the poor who were rich in faith.

We can be equally guilty in our generation. Would not most of us feel greatly honored if some renowned entertainer were to be a guest in our home? Never mind the corruptness of his movies or the filthiness of his songs. This is a real celebrity and he has come to **our** house. How flattered we would be! What pride we would feel as we told our friends of the honor that was ours.

We heap great honor on well-known sports figures with little regard for what they are morally or spiritually. We go out of our way to become acquainted with politicians and find great pleasure in "name dropping." We hardly seem aware of the glory we bestow on the very people who are undermining the moral fiber of our nation and are wielding a corrupting influence in our own lives and in the lives of our children.

Why did the Christians of James' day look up to the rich? Why do we tend to do the same? The answer surely must be found in our own misplaced priorities. We give lip service to the foolishness of gaining the whole world at the expense of one's soul, while deep down we glorify fame, fortune, and pleasure. Intellectually, we understand that true success in life is to be measured in terms of one's preparation for eternity, but find it difficult to remove from our hearts the world's concepts of success and greatness. We do not mean to imply that all the rich and famous are corrupt (such would not be true), but we are saying that misplaced priorities can blind us to the corrupting influence that wickedness and filth in high places can have upon our own souls.

The great people of James' day were not the skilled participants in the Roman games, the military giants, or the Caesars. Whatever honor was to be rendered to such men was the honor that attended the office they held (Rom 13.7). The great people of that day were such people as Barnabas, Dorcas, Mary, Timothy, Peter, and Paul. The truly great people of our day are those who are faithful in service to God and man. We worship with some of them every Lord's day. Our homes can be honored by their presence on almost any day. They are men and women "of whom the world [is] not worthy." Let us recognize their greatness, learn to truly love and appreciate them, and give to them the honor they are due.

On the Outside Looking In

Our seven year old could hardly wait to get to Canada where she could ride a bus to school. Often she had looked at those big, yellow buses packed with children and had thought how much she was losing in life because she wasn't riding some bus like that. All the excitement was on the inside, and she was on the outside looking in. Our move to Canada is now complete. For three months she has ridden that bus to school, and is learning an important lesson: what seems so exciting when you are on the outside looking in often proves to be but an illusion; the reality never quite equals the dream.

So it is in spiritual realms. We wonder how many Christians, born and raised "in the church," feel that they have been deprived by their early training of the real fun in life; that surely the truly "good times" are to be had in the world with its dance halls, night spots, bawdy parties, and exciting affairs. Their convictions being too strong and the pressures too great for them actually to engage in such activities, they stand on the outside looking somewhat longingly within. If only they could realize that the fruit of such conduct is indescribably bitter, and, besides, that the reality never quite equals the dream. If only they would listen to a "prodigal son" of our generation, they would learn that sin's promises are not only an illusion, but a very cruel illusion at that.

We wonder how many people in faithful churches are impressed with the big, promotional programs and inflated statistics of more "progressive" churches, and in turn feel a tinge of embarrassment over the scriptural, but sometimes "lackluster" efforts of the congregation of which they are a part. One only needs to observe the cyclical and temporary nature of such programs to realize that there is in them nothing of permanent value, but they can seem so thrilling when one is on the outside looking in.

What is needed is faith: faith to accept that God's word is complete, furnishing us to every good work (2 Tim 3.16-17); faith to accept that God's plan is best, and that while his plan may not be so exciting to human eyes (the gospel works like leaven, not like dynamite), it cannot be improved upon through human wisdom and ingenuity; faith to accept that the gospel's promises are not illusory as are the world's, but that what God "had promised He [is] also able to perform"(Rom 4.21); faith to accept that God's word provides the only true formula for a happy and fulfilled life; faith to accept that eternal life and happiness are far more to be desired than the pleasures and excitement of this world; faith to accept that God knows best in everything.

Don't be deceived! Don't look with envy on the world with its riches and pleasure! If you are a Christian—not only in name, but in life and affection—you have within your grasp the greatest happiness and fulfillment that can be obtained in this life.

Super-Christians

Beware those who boast of superior spiritual qualities or intellectual abilities. Their conduct will invariably bring grief.

A young dating couple goes on a weekend trip together. They plan to stay in the same motel room, but will sleep in separate beds. They really don't understand the fuss. They are aware of the terribleness of sin. They know the pitfalls that fornication presents. They have given their lives to Christ. They can handle any temptation that might arise.

A man in the congregation grows weary of the simple gospel lessons he hears Sunday after Sunday. He longs for something deep, something that will challenge his intellect. When he gets the chance to teach a Bible class, he gives the class something to chew on. None of that same old repetitious material from the book of Acts or life of Christ will ever be discussed in his class.

A married woman is constantly in the presence of a single man. Wherever she is, the young man will be right by her side. But don't worry. They are people of great spirituality and will profit greatly from each other's spiritual qualities.

We are not dealing with the hypothetical; these are real live people we have described. And the sad truth is that their likes are found in congregations across the nation, creating trouble and causing misery among the faithful to the Lord.

Their counterpart appears in the scriptures in the form of the Corinthians (1 Cor 8.1-13), who gloried in their superior knowledge; who were so "strong" that they could go into an idol's temple and eat of idolatrous feasts; who thought they were beyond falling; who couldn't worry about the spiritual weaklings in the church who might be led into sin by their conduct; who were apparently motivated by the "after all, such people ought to grow up and quit being so weak—the church would probably be better off without them anyway" attitude.

It is interesting to observe that Paul was not very impressed with this air of spirituality and knowledge manifested by these Corinthians. To them he wrote, "Knowledge puffs up, but love edifies" (8.1), and, further, you know "nothing yet as [you] ought to know" (8.2). He reminded them that the weak brother being destroyed by their "knowledge" was one "for whom Christ died" (8.11). In contrast to their arrogance, he spoke of his own actions in buffeting his body, and bringing it into bondage…lest he himself should be rejected (9.27). Then in one final warning he said, "Therefore let him who thinks be stands take heed lest he fall" (10.12).

If you find yourself among those described above, we urge you to repent. If you are not among them, beware of those who are, and "restore [them] in a spirit of gentleness." Indeed, "Pride goes before destruction and a haughty spirit before a fall" (Prov 16.18).

Living with Criticism

From the *Reader's Digest* we lift this quote, authored by Roger Rosenblatt: "I have seen many amazing things in my life, but I have never seen anyone who could take criticism well. All criticism, be it casual or vicious or constructive, is unpalatable. Sure, you can profit from criticism in the long and painful run. But taking it is something else. Taking it means letting it go down like custard—no blinking, no flinching, no wishing you were dead."

How true! But I'm glad my critics have not always been silent. "You are a good preacher, but you repeat yourself too much," a man told me when I first started preaching. It didn't "go down like custard," and I'm not sure my "thank you" was as sincere as it ought to have been, but I tried harder after that not to repeat myself unnecessarily. "You sing so loud you give me a headache," a lady complained on another occasion. Ouch! That one hurt worse than her headache. But, I did need to moderate the volume.

Some criticism is dishonest. Judas' criticism of Mary had a noble ring to it: "Why was this fragrant oil not sold...and given to the poor?" (John 12.5). But it was dishonest, and the noble ring was only an intentional disguise to hide his dishonest purposes. Moreover, the criticism would not have been valid even if it had been honest. With Jesus' help Mary was able to ignore this bit of criticism. Similarly, there are times when we should ignore criticism. I wish I could always discern when.

The way criticism is offered makes a big difference. If I must be criticized, make the criticism brief and to the point, and then drop it. Criticism that is repeated again and again becomes nagging, and nagging usually produces stubbornness rather than improvement. Don't act like you are joking when you are criticizing. It is true, too, that "a spoonful of sugar helps the medicine go down." Don't set me up for the "kill," but a sincere expression of appreciation offered with the criticism makes the "medicine" a little easier to take. If you feel no appreciation for me, you probably should leave the criticizing to someone who does.

I have known people who could profit from criticism and continue to love their critics, and I have admired them. Peter was that kind of man. In fact, his ability to accept criticism was a major factor in the greatness he attained.

The Holy Spirit has something to say on this subject: "Do not correct a scoffer, lest he hate you; rebuke a wise man, and he will love you" (Prov 9.8). Exactly! The true fiber of a man may well be determined by his ability to accept criticism.

So, if you must be a critic, learn how to soften the blow while at the same time being forthright. Always be honest. And, if you must be criticized, have the humility to make necessary corrections. As long as the world stands there will be criticism. Let's learn to live with it graciously.

Plenteous in Mercy

In studying the relationship which existed between Jesus and His apostles, we marvel at two facts: (1) the weakness of the apostles, and (2) the patience of Jesus.

The apostles were truly weak and blundering men. Jesus told them again and again of the spiritual nature of His kingdom, but they still looked for an earthly kingdom and childishly argued over which of them would be the greatest. He tried to prepare them for His crucifixion, but they never understood. He performed great miracles before them, but they could still be frightened even when He was in their midst. He often had to say, "O ye of little faith."

There was Peter: speaking when he should have been silent, sinking in the sea, asleep when he should have been praying, cutting off Malchus' ear, following afar off, and denying Jesus.

Yet, despite all of Peter's blunders, one can never doubt Peter's love for the Lord, his faith in Him as the Son of God, or his desire to please Him. In response to Jesus' question, "Do you also want to go away?" Peter blurted out, "Lord, to whom shall we go? You have the words of eternal life" (John 6.67-68). Truly words fitly spoken! Peter in his impetuous moments could say the wrong things, and in his weakness he could sin, but he loved the Lord and was not about to leave Him. He was always willing to accept the Lord's rebukes, and could weep bitterly when he did sin. And so it was with the other apostles.

Lesser men would have despaired, giving up on these weak, frail, stumbling disciples. But not our Lord. He was not so concerned with what they were then as with what they could become. And through His patience He transformed them into the strongest men this world has ever known. He rebuked and chastened them, but they never questioned His love nor doubted that they belonged to Him. They had been given to Him of God, and He had kept every one of them—except Judas (John 17.12).

Except Judas! The "son of perdition"! The Lord's patience had to be cut off toward him, for he had turned his back on the Lord, apostatized, and refused the Lord's rebuke and chastening. And the Lord gave him up!

Can we not see God's attitude toward us as we observe Jesus and His apostles? Jesus upon earth was "God with us" (Matt 1.23), "the image of the invisible God" (Col 1.15), "the brightness of His glory and the express image of His person" (Heb 1.3). The attitude which Jesus demonstrated toward the apostles in their weaknesses is the same attitude which God has toward us in our weaknesses. We must never question. His love and patience toward those who live by His teaching, accept His chastening and rebukes, and repenting, constantly seek His forgiveness. And we must never question His ability to transform us (Yes, even me!) into the strong, useful servants He wants us to be. "The LORD is merciful and gracious, slow to anger and abounding in mercy" (Psa 103.8).

Thinking of Quitting?

No doubt, someone will read this article that is discouraged, weary of struggling, disappointed in his brethren, facing severe obstacles in his service to the Lord, and is in danger of quitting. But I would make this appeal: "Before you quit, look anew at the incentives the Lord holds before you; look again at heaven."

Heaven means victory—victory in the strife with Satan and his allies. The battle is sometimes hard; the foe is formidable. Our own strength seems so small. We become discouraged. But lift our eyes! On our side is the Lord, the One who has already won the battle (Gen 3.15). With His aid we can be victorious. We can be "more than conquerors through Him who loved us" (Rom 8.37).

Heaven means beauty—unsurpassed beauty—a street of gold, walls of jasper, a foundation of precious stones, gates of pearl, a crystal clear river flowing from the throne of God.

Heaven means home—Happiness is not found in our material surroundings, but in being with those we love. We experience homesickness, but our homesickness is not for a house or anything material, but for wife and children, for loved ones. Similarly, we speak of the beauty of heaven, and truly its beauty enhances our anticipation, but surely the greatest joy will be found in being with our Lord, the One "whom having not seen [we] love," and with our God, with the Spirit, with the angels, and with the redeemed of all ages. This will be our eternal homecoming.

Heaven means happiness—there will be nothing there to mar our happiness. There will be no more tears, no more sickness, no more heartache, no more death, "nor sorrow, nor crying. There shall be no more pain, for the former things have passed away" (Rev 21.4).

Heaven means holiness—never again will we hear the name of our Lord taken in vain. There will be no more adultery, filth, guilt, murder, crime. Truth will abound. There will be no more lying, deceit, flattery, hypocrisy. Women will no longer have to fear those who would abuse and desecrate them. Love will be pure and unfeigned. The Lord assures us, "But there shall by no means enter it anything that defiles, or causes an abomination or a lie, but only those who are written in the Lamb's Book of Life" (Rev 21.27).

Heaven means eternity—this blessed state shall never end. "When we've been there ten thousand years, Bright shining as the sun, We've no less days to sing God's praise than when we first begun" (Joseph Scriven).

You can quit if you so choose, for God will not force anyone to serve Him. But, remember, the day you quit is the day you forfeit all hope of eternal happiness and choose in its place eternal damnation. And eternity is a long time.

Considering the Outcome

We have no sympathy for those who at every funeral "preach the dead right on into heaven," who ignore the obvious failure on the part of the deceased to serve the Lord, who try to think that all will somehow get to heaven in spite of their disobedience. There is a hell, and the many of this earth (in contrast to the few) are going there (Matt 7.13-14).

But we must not allow one extreme to beget another. While the majority will be lost, there are those in this world whose single purpose in life is to serve the Lord and go to heaven when they die; who devote themselves daily to studying God's word and living by its precepts. When such people die it is right to speak of their good life and faithfulness to the Lord; it is right to hold out hope to their loved ones; it is right to commend their example of faithfulness and perseverance to those who may be discouraged; it is right to speak of their eternal reward.

The Hebrew writer stated it this way: "Remember those who led you, who spoke the word of God to you; and considering the result of their conduct, imitate their faith" (Heb 13.7-NASB). Three things are implied in this verse: (1) There had been men in their midst who had served the Lord faithfully unto death. (2) The Hebrew Christians were to be confident that the outcome of the lives of those men was a happy one. (3) Considering this, they were to imitate their faith.

We, like the Hebrews, have had the good fortune of knowing many who have lived godly lives and have now passed on to their reward. Some were elders; some were preachers; some were Bible class teachers; others were just good, faithful, dependable disciples of the Lord who placed His kingdom first in their lives. We are not speaking of the lukewarm and indifferent. We are not speaking of those who claim to be Christians, but were lacking in the fruits of Christianity. We are speaking of the truly dedicated ones who constantly reflected the character of their Father and their Lord Jesus Christ. Their influence on our lives was tremendous. They were men and women of whom this world was not worthy. And the list grows with each passing year.

Every one of these had to overcome serious obstacles to be faithful to the Lord. The Devil challenged each one of them, but he failed. They gained the victory through Christ. Now they are eternally happy because they persevered. Could we ask any one of them, "Was it worth it?" his reply immediately would be, "It was a thousand times worth it!" Not one of them regrets a single moment he spent in the Lord's service.

We thank God for such people. We rejoice in their salvation. We look on their passing not as those "who have no hope." And "considering the result of their conduct," we dedicate ourselves to imitating their faith.

Hope Is to Be Found in Christ

"I wish I could think that I have come just a short distance toward becoming as prepared as he was," a woman said to me recently concerning a man who had died. Her statement was intended to be an expression of confidence in the deceased, and I shared her confidence, but the truth is: if that lady is living a faithful life in Christ, she is fully as prepared as any other person in Christ.

Entrance into heaven will not be based upon a long list of credentials built up cumulatively through the years (so many new converts, so many passages memorized, so many lives influenced, so many years in the service of the Lord, so many sermons preached, etc.), the person's chances of going to heaven being enhanced with each new credential. Entrance into heaven will be based on the merit of Christ's blood. One prepares for heaven by entering into Christ through faith, repentance, and baptism (Gal 3.27; Rom 6.3); living a faithful life in Christ; and dying in Christ. "Blessed are the dead who die in the Lord" (Rev 14.13). This is the true basis for one's hope, whether he has been a faithful Christian for fifty years or is just rising from baptism in newness of life.

Now if the lady had said, "I wish I could think that I have come just a short distance toward being as God like as I believe he was," that would have been different. Here is the prevailing purpose of every Christian, to become more like God every day. "And everyone **who has this hope** in Him purifies himself, just as He is pure" (1 John 3.3). Regular worship, liberal giving, unceasing prayer, concerned benevolence, unfeigned love of the brethren, self-control, etc.—all of which are commanded of God—are a means to the end of becoming like Him, or as stated by Jesus, "That you may be the sons of your Father in heaven" (Matt 5.45). One who ignores these commands shows his contempt for God, becomes unfaithful, ceases to be like God, and loses his hope of heaven. On the other hand, one who does conscientiously obey the commands of God becomes more God-like, and the person who has done so for fifty years will obviously have attained a greater degree of God-likeness than one who has just begun the Christian life. But while we recognize different levels in attainment toward becoming like God, all who are **faithful,** and are thus purifying themselves as He is pure, share **equally** the hope of heaven. None has earned his way to heaven. All are dependent on God's grace, and His grace is extended to all the faithful.

Let not the young in the faith, then, be intimidated by the attainments of the more mature in the faith. Let not the mature become proud and overconfident. All must be faithful. All must be growing. All must become more and more like God. And all must die in the Lord. And to all who do so, the Lord will say, "Well done good and **faithful** servant; you have been **faithful** over a few things, I will make you ruler over many things. Enter into the joy of your lord."

They Can't Live It

Many who have never entered the Lord's service explain their hesitancy with the words, "I'm afraid I just can't live it." We usually try to quell their fears, but the truth is, **they can't live it**, for their concept of what **it** is they are trying to live is a completely false concept.

Consider the man whose wife became a Christian. He was sure she couldn't "live it." He watched her carefully, and sure enough, one day under considerable stress, she lost control, yelled at the children, and said some things a Christian ought not to say. "If she were a Christian," the man thought, "she wouldn't talk like that; I knew she couldn't live it." On another day the preacher came around, and in reaction to something someone said, he turned a bit red, although he otherwise controlled his temper. But the man saw that tinge of redness, and immediately concluded, "That preacher can't live it either." He eventually observed faults in other Christians, and finally concluded that none of them could "live it," that the whole church was a bunch of hypocrites. Of course he never even tried, for he knew his weaknesses all too well. He **knew** he couldn't "live it."

Poor man! He thinks that the Christian life is a life of perfection; that all "Christians" fall into one of two categories: either they are perfect or they are hypocrites. He knows he can't live up to perfection, to the standards he has set for others, and is thinking with an almost self-righteous attitude, "One thing about it, Preacher, I'm not going to be a hypocrite."

But there is pardon for the sincere Christian's imperfections. "If anyone sins, we have an Advocate with the Father, Jesus Christ the righteous" (1 John 2.1). And that Christian who sincerely strives to live for the Lord, and daily seeks His forgiveness, **though he should have a thousand weaknesses**, is no hypocrite. There are hypocrites in the church, and we offer no defense in their behalf. But weaknesses do not necessarily imply hypocrisy.

Let the faithful Christian, then, not be intimidated by the constant charge of "hypocrites in the church." And let the sinner forget about living "it," if by "it" he means perfection, and let him come to Christ, through whom he **can** go to heaven.

Discouraged of Men

We recently read a very fine article by J.D. Jeffcoat entitled *"Discourager of Men."* Indeed, churches everywhere are troubled by those who are constantly discouraging others. But something needs to be said also concerning those who allow themselves to be discouraged.

Some are discouraged by criticism. Every person who has tried to do God's will has been criticized. Jesus was constantly criticized. So was Moses. Paul once said, "All those in Asia have turned away from me" (2 Tim 1.15), and apparently he was afraid that Timothy might be affected by this adverse criticism against Paul (2 Tim 1.8). Do you listen to others when they criticize you? Do you listen when they criticize the local church of which you are a part or some good person within the congregation? Do you allow their negative comments to affect your feelings? Or do you cast aside their discouraging remarks that you might maintain a positive attitude toward the Lord, His church, and His work?

Criticism may be just. But, on the other hand, it may be an outgrowth of envy toward others; or it may be a dishonest effort to destroy another; or it may just be the product of ignorance as to what is right and wrong, consequently ignorance of what deserves criticism and what deserves praise. One must not be discouraged in the Lord's work by unjust criticism.

Others are discouraged by the chronic pessimist. This is the man who is always reminding the church that "it won't do any good," and that "this is just a hard area and we're never going to convert people here." He can in one business meeting totally demoralize a whole church, and can destroy in one sitting that which took a year to build up. He is the true "discourager of men." But if he is wrong in discouraging, others are wrong in allowing themselves to be discouraged by his pessimistic remarks.

The apostles serve as a perfect example of men who refused to be discouraged. They were constantly faced with setbacks; their teaching was attacked; they suffered from those within and from those without. It was said of them: "To the present hour we both hunger and thirst, and we are poorly clothed, and beaten, and homeless. And we labor, working with our own hands. Being reviled, we bless; being persecuted, we endure; being defamed, we entreat. We have been made as the filth of the world, the off scouring of all things until now" (1 Cor 4.11-13). **But they kept on preaching**!

Blessed is that man who is not easily discouraged by others; who can see through unworthy criticism for what it really is; who takes his stand for truth and right and does not let others move him from that stand. Let us avoid being either a "discourager of men" or "discouraged of men." Rather, let us be found working for the Lord, encouraging and finding encouragement in the hope we have in Christ.

The Key to Contentment

"And having food and clothing, with these we shall be content," the apostle said (1 Tim 6.8); but the Lord may never have given a command harder for twentieth century Christians to obey.

The secret to contentment can be seen in the beautiful character of Ruth. Far away from home and with few provisions, she did not complain, but rather determined to pursue the one available means of providing for herself and her mother-in-law—the lowly, but legitimate, task of gleaning. Commenting on Ruth's decision, *Pulpit Commentary* says this of Ruth: "When she could not lift up her circumstances to her mind, (she) brought down her mind to her circumstances."

She brought down her mind to her circumstances! There is the key. If I can't afford a Cadillac, then I need to bring my mind down to be thankful for the Reliant that I do drive; if I can't afford to eat out three times a week, then I need to bring my mind down to enjoy the occasional dining out that I can afford; if I can't afford $150 worth of long-distance phone calls per month, then I must be grateful that there is still a postal service and bring my mind down to writing letters. And so with the clothing I wear, the house I live in, the recreation I enjoy, etc.

We do not find happiness or godliness in looking longingly at what everybody else can afford; we find only misery and ingratitude. We do not have to look far to find wives who are unhappy with the circumstances their husbands can afford, or children who feel deprived because of the circumstances their parents can afford, or preachers who are miserable and looking to other employment because of their discontent with the salaries churches are able or willing to pay. While we acknowledge that there is a line below which one cannot live comfortably, for most of these, happiness is in reach. They need only to bring their minds down to their circumstances.

Let no one think that such contentment comes automatically. Paul said that he had **learned** "in whatever state I am, to be content" (Phil 4.10-13). And he had learned that lesson well. He could "bring his mind down" to circumstances that would include a Roman prison and "wants" that needed to be supplied. He could be content when full or when hungry, when abounding, or when suffering need. Paul's contentment under such circumstances makes us ashamed of our own discontent; and when he speaks of the true source of his contentment, he brings us to question our own spirituality: "I can do all things through Christ who strengthens me."

So, whether we be rich or poor in this world's goods, let us turn to the Lord, learn through Him to bring our minds down to our circumstances, and thereby discover how truly "rich" we really are … and then be content. Let us experience the realization that "godliness with contentment is great gain" (1Tim 6.6).

The Church Not Found in the Bible

The word "church" is used in two senses in the Bible. (1) It is used in the **universal sense**, referring to the saved of all ages, and (2) it is used in the **local sense**, referring to a congregation of saved people in any given locality.

So, we read of Jesus' giving Himself for the church (Eph 5.25) and of His purchasing the church with His own blood (Acts 20.28). In these two passages the word "church" is used in the universal sense. Jesus gave Himself for the saved of all ages and purchased them with His own blood.

But we also read of the church in Corinth (1 Cor 1.2), the church in Jerusalem (Acts 11.22), and the seven churches of Asia (Rev 1.11). The reference in these passages is to congregations of saved people in these different localities. These local churches were organized, each with its own "bishops and deacons" (Phil 1.1).

The Bible does not use the word "church," however, in the **denominational sense**. One cannot read in the scriptures of denominational conferences, associations, or synods. Nor can he read of denominational hierarchies, names, creeds, or doctrines. These are the inventions of men, not of God. They have been the cause of many problems in religion.

What of the reader? Does he consider himself a part of that universal church made up of all the saved? Is he also a member of a local church? Does his membership in that local church bring him also into an association with a denominational organization—an organization **bigger** than the local church, but **smaller** than the universal church? If so, he is a part of a "church" not found in the Bible.

It must be our goal just to convert people to Jesus Christ, bring them to salvation through Him, and lead them to affiliation with a local church that is a part of no denominational organization—a local church that is organized as were the local churches of the scriptures. This is the Bible way. Why should we continue to perpetuate that which God never founded nor authorized in His word, the Bible?

No Central Ruling Body

We frequently come in contact with people who cannot understand how churches of Christ function without some central ruling body to hold them in line. "You have one church believing one thing over here, and another church believing something else over there; you have so many differences among your churches," they say.

The fallacy in that statement lies within the fact that "**I**" don't have a church "over here" and one "over there." The church of Christ is not to be viewed as a conglomerate of local churches, the conglomerate having so many schools, so many religious papers, so many members in so many churches. I am not a part of any such conglomerate and no one should be.

As a Christian, I am a part of two things. (1) I am a part of a **heavenly body**, Christ's church, made up of all of God's saved people throughout the ages—some still on earth, others in Paradise. This heavenly body has no schools, no papers, no organizations. God alone knows how many make up this great body. (2) I am a part of a **local church**, some of whom (I trust) are parts of that heavenly body and some of whom very likely are not. Similar local churches exist throughout the world, but each stands as a separate entity under the authority of Jesus Christ, the chief Shepherd (1 Peter 5.4). But they are not **my** churches; nor am I a part of any of them.

The local church of which I am a part looks to Christ (through the New Testament) for its instructions, not to some central ruling body. If that local church ceases to be in agreement with Christ, **He** will remove it, no longer considering it His (Rev 2.5); it will not be removed by some central ruling body or by some other local church or group of churches. If there are dissimilarities between churches that refer to themselves as "churches of Christ," it is because some are no longer in agreement with Christ. Christ removes those churches that are not in agreement with Him, but since they are not "my" churches and I am not a part of them, I bear no responsibility in that decision. My responsibility, then, is to serve the Lord faithfully as a part of His heavenly body; to encourage other Christians, **wherever they are**, to be faithful to Christ; and to help maintain the local church of which I am a part as a faithful church of Christ.

Now, having explained this, we would ask our querists: Would you rather be a part of a local church that looks to a central ruling body for its instructions or of one that looks only to Jesus Christ for its instructions? Would you rather be a part of a local church that can be removed by a central ruling body, made up of fallible men, or of one that can only be removed by Jesus Christ? Of greater importance, of which would **Christ** want you to be a part? It is wonderful to have brothers and sisters in Christ all over the world, but my relationship with them is through a common relationship with Christ, not through some central ruling body or conglomerate of churches.

What a Fellowship!

"Does the church of Christ have a high priest?" the young Mormon "sister" asked. "Yes," was our emphatic answer. "Does the church of Christ have apostles?" Again, "Yes" was our answer.

We have no doubt that our answer was correct, but we seem naturally inclined to give an opposite answer. Our concepts of the Lord's church can be so narrow. We speak of the "universal church," and think only of the living saints throughout the world. But the Lord's church is unlimited in time or place. It is all Christians of all ages. Some are on earth; some in Paradise; but all are a part of the Lord's church.

When we obeyed the gospel, the Lord saved us, and added us to His body. Here we have fellowship with Barnabas, Stephen, Dorcas, Peter, and other great characters of the scriptures (Heb 12.22-24). Here we have fellowship with the wonderful saints whom we have known in our lifetime who have already departed "to be with the Lord." Here we have fellowship with the Christians on earth today, some known, and some unknown. This is the church of Christ. It is the Lord's purchased people, purchased with His own blood (Acts 20.28).

"Did the Lord's church cease to exist during the Dark Ages?" someone asks. No! No! We know little about those who lived on earth during that period. But for the Lord's church to have ceased to exist, the devil would have had to somehow enter paradise and destroy completely those faithful ones who had gone on. Remember, they are a part of this great body.

"How many members are there of the church of Christ?" Only God knows. We surely couldn't arrive at an accurate figure by adding up all who worship with "known" local churches over the world. This would exclude the faithful who have already passed on. Besides, there may be faithful Christians meeting in some remote area unknown to any other faithful Christians. And, of course, God only knows who are truly faithful and thus truly constitute His church.

Who is the church's high priest? It is Jesus Christ, the One "called by God" (Heb 5.4-5), perfected through suffering (Heb 5.7-9), now "passed through the heavens" and sitting "at the right hand of God" (Heb 4.14-16; 10.10-12), having offered His own blood as an atonement for our sins (Heb 9.11-12). Who are the church's apostles? They are Peter, Andrew, James, John, Philip, etc. These are the specially chosen ambassadors who speak officially for the King, and they still speak to the Lord's church through the scriptures. They are **our** apostles, too.

Are we too worldly to appreciate what we have in Christ? Can we not lift ourselves above this world with its narrow concepts to see ourselves as a part of a great body that reaches from earth into Paradise and even into heaven itself? We all sit together with Christ "in the heavenly places." What a fellowship! What a glorious privilege!

Good Churches Have Problems

"No internal problems," the man said. And our first reaction was that of admiration for this "ideal" church that knew no problems. But with further observation our thinking changed.

The Bible speaks of a church that had "no problems." The church at Laodicea was "rich, and had become wealthy, and had need of nothing" (Rev 3.17). On the other hand the Jerusalem church was faced with several problems. They had to witness the death of a hypocritical, lying couple (Acts 5.1-11). There was murmuring because of neglect of the Grecian widows (Acts 6.1-7). There were doctrinal problems over the question of circumcision (Acts 11.1-18; 15.4-5). Jerusalem had its problems while Laodicea was "free of problems"—yet every Bible student knows that Jerusalem was the approved church while Laodicea was nauseating to the Lord.

Further, when one observes the problems of the Jerusalem church, he recognizes the problems were a direct outgrowth of the **work and activity** of that congregation. Had there not been the spirit of benevolence that prevailed among its members, there would have been no occasion for Ananias and Sapphira's lie or for the murmuring over neglect. Had there been no evangelization among the Gentiles, there would have been no problem over circumcision. Jerusalem had problems **because** they were a working, active, thriving, growing church. And it may well be that Laodicea's absence of problems was a direct outgrowth of its **lukewarmness** and lack of vitality.

We conclude that a lazy, "do nothing" church may well be free of problems, but an active, working church can expect certain problems. A church that succeeds in converting alcoholics, drug addicts, divorcees; that seeks a "Samaritan woman" of our day, or a "Simon the sorcerer," or a "Mary Magdalene" can anticipate some problems.

But that church which chooses the alternative, preaching to and converting only the morally good who fit well into their own social and economic circles, while avoiding some problems, faces the greatest problem of all in their failure to obey the commandment of the Lord (Mark 16.15) and to follow His own personal example. A church that develops thinking people who objectively study every Bible question for themselves can expect some differences to arise in their earnest search for truth. A hospitable church must be prepared for charges of neglect in their show of hospitality. True zeal for the Lord will beget problems but woe to that church that neglects the Lord's work in order to avoid problems. The Lord's anathema is upon that church.

It's not the existence or non-existence of problems, then, that determines the strength of a church, but how the church deals with its problems. Love for one another, mutual concern, longsuffering, humility, love for truth, determination to do God's will—these are the qualities that make for a strong church. They cannot stop problems from developing, but they can enable a church to bring its problems to God-approved solutions.

The Booing Spectators

Have you ever noticed who does the booing at a ball game? It's not the players on the field. They have made their own mistakes and they are not inclined to boo their fellow-player when he makes his. They are pulling for one another, encouraging, helpful. They play as a team, win or lose as a team, suffer together as a team, rejoice together as a team. It is the spectators who boo. So it is in every walk of life: it is the spectators who, as a rule, do the criticizing, not the participants.

Unfortunately, in every congregation there are the spectators and the participants. The spectators never teach a Bible class, preach, lead singing, or preside at the table; they really don't get that much involved in the worship itself. But more often than not, they are the very ones who are found criticizing the preacher or song leader or Bible class teacher. They are the ones who are so embarrassed and incensed when someone inadvertently commits an "error" in his efforts to lead the group. They come wanting to hear something that is interesting and that will make the time fly by. If they hear it, they "cheer;" if not they "boo."

Not so with the true participants, those who are really involved in the Lord's work. They are the ones "cheering on" that "rookie" who is preaching his first sermon or leading his first song. When a brother attempts to teach his first Bible class, they are looking for ways to be helpful. They are sympathetic; they rejoice in the success of others; they mourn over the sorrows of others; they feel for the one who has failed, make allowances for him, encourage him to try again, and assure him that he will do better next time. They rejoice especially in the development of the young men and women in the Lord's work. They are just as nervous and excited when the young people make their first attempt at presiding at the table or teaching a class as they would be if it were their own children.

How many preachers have decided to move because of the booing spectators' right at the time when the participants were enjoying their greatest spiritual growth? How many elders have planned the work around the demands of the spectators rather than the needs of the participants?

Spectators need to become participants and find out what it's like out there "on the field." Participants need to keep on doing their best, ignoring the "boos" while looking to their all-seeing and understanding "Manager" for approval. All need to be preparing for judgment, where it will be the "doers of the word," not the critics, who will be saved. "Finally, all of you be of one mind, having compassion for one another; love as brothers, be tenderhearted, be courteous" (1 Pet 3.8).

Christians, like ballplayers, make a sad mistake when they listen too closely to the "boo-birds."

Improving Our Worship

Our lack of fervency and reverence in worship is a matter of grave concern to all spiritually-minded people. We have often caught ourselves singing, but not worshiping; bowing our heads, but not praying; sitting through a sermon, but not participating in a study of God's word. Such action is mockery, bringing condemnation on the "worshiper" rather than God's approval.

What is the solution to the problem? Some have sought for the solution in spontaneous singing and chain prayers. A group meets for a devotional period. No song numbers are announced; somebody (anybody) just starts a song, and everybody joins in. Instead of one person leading the prayer, all the men take part, each one adding his little bit until the last man in the circle gives the final "Amen." The purpose behind this practice is to help people feel closer to God as they worship.

I am not questioning the scripturalness of these practices, but if someone thinks they hold the solution to our problems of worship, I believe him to be absolutely wrong. Or if such practices lead the participants to look disdainfully on "led" singing or "led" prayers, considering such to be an inferior way of worship, they become downright dangerous. Improvement in worship is not brought about by changing the order or externals of worship, but by changing the hearts of men. It comes from stronger faith and greater love for the Lord.

When we come to love the Lord and appreciate His sacrifice as we ought, such words as, "I stand amazed in the presence of Jesus the Nazarene, and wonder how He could love me, a sinner condemned, unclean," will awaken an immediate response in our hearts, so that with genuine fervor we will sing, "How marvelous! How wonderful! And my song shall ever be; How marvelous! How wonderful! Is my Savior's love for me." And whether the song is sung spontaneously or is announced and led by a song leader will become a matter of indifference.

When we develop a true consciousness of God—a consciousness of His greatness, His presence, His concern, His love, His awareness, His listening ear—and an appreciation of our own littleness and unworthiness, we will begin praying as we ought.

Spontaneous singing and chain prayers only provide temporary help in treating the symptom. But what we need is to get to the root of our problems, our own lack of faith and love for the Lord.

We shall try, but we will never in this life reach perfection in worship. But one day we shall see our Lord. A consciousness of what He has done for us will sweep our souls as never before. An awareness of our hopelessness, were it not for Him, will stir our spirits. And then—and possibly only then—we will break forth in praise with the sincere adoration which He deserves. And we are quite sure it won't take any artificial form or arrangement of worship to prompt that bursting forth of praise.

Do You Pray?

The worshiper who would pray in the assembly must do more than bow his head and close his eyes. He must pray. "Otherwise, if you bless with the spirit, how will he who occupies the place of the uninformed say 'Amen' at your giving of thanks, since he does not understand what you say?" (1 Cor 14.16) This verse suggests four requirements if one is to enter into a prayer.

1. **He must listen to the prayer.** One cannot legitimately say "Amen" at the conclusion of a prayer if he has not listened to the prayer. "Mind wandering" is an ever-present problem. We sing, but we don't observe the words of the song. We bow our heads, but we don't listen to the prayer. We sit through the sermon, but our minds wander to things of an earthly nature. Consequently, we attend worship periods, but we don't worship as we ought. If one is to pray, with the congregation, he must listen to the prayer.

2. **He must understand the prayer.** When a man in the first century led a prayer in an unknown tongue, the worshiper could not say "Amen," for he could not understand the language in which the prayer was spoken. Neither can the worshiper say "Amen" today if the leader has not spoken loudly enough to be heard or if he has used words or phrases which the worshiper does not understand. Those who lead prayers in the assembly should be conscious of the needs of the whole congregation, speaking up where all can hear and using words which all can understand.

3. **He must agree with the prayer.** A number of years ago, while sitting beside an older preacher, I observed his saying "Yes" or "Yes, Lord" at the conclusion of each separate phrase of the prayer as it was being led. He spoke the words softly enough that I was probably the only one in the assembly who could hear them, but I was impressed. Obviously, this brother was listening to every phrase, determining whether or not he agreed with the phrase, and was then softly speaking his agreement. He was not just sitting through a prayer; he was praying. Occasionally we hear sentiments expressed in prayer with which we do not agree. To these sentiments we cannot say "Amen."

4. **He must say "Amen."** The word "Amen" means "so let it be." We long to hear the strong, resounding "Amen" at the close of prayers which we used to hear. We fear that the move away from this practice is just another step toward cold, lifeless formality in our worship periods. We are not contending, however, that one must say the word "Amen" audibly; but we are suggesting that at least in his mind he should say "Amen," thus making the prayer his own prayer. He has listened to the prayer; he has understood the prayer; he has agreed with the prayer; now he speaks to God his "Amen" or approval of the prayer as his prayer. In this manner he unites with other worshipers in common prayer unto God.

Wasting Time in Bible Class

We are becoming increasingly alarmed at the time wasted in Bible classes discussing matters of no importance. Recently, in a study of the "man of sin" (2 Thes 2), we heard a teacher ask about the hindering force that had held back the man of sin. The class must have spent fifteen minutes discussing that question. Answers ranged from the dogmatic to the "I think so" and the "could it have been."

The truth is, we don't know what that hindering force was. God didn't tell us. Consequently, it doesn't really matter, for had it mattered, He who has given us "all things that pertain to life and godliness" would have given us that information, too. It is one of those questions like, "Why did Nicodemus come by night?" or, "What was Paul's thorn in the flesh?" or, "What color were the horses that pulled the eunuch's chariot?" Time spent in discussing such questions is wasted time.

"The secret things belong to the Lord our God, but those things which are revealed belong to us and to our children forever, that we may do all the words of this law" (Deut 29.29).

We must teach and preach with exclamation points, not question marks. We must preach the word, not our opinions or "think sos" or "could it have beens" or "it might bes." "But avoid foolish and ignorant disputes, knowing that they generate strife" (2 Tim 2.23).

Now I'm not planning to withdraw from the teacher mentioned above, for that teacher happens also to be the writer of this article. Somehow I find it easy to be patient with him. But I am ordering him a good supply of sackcloth and ashes, and I'm forcing him to resolve never to do it again. And I hope his resolution will encourage other teachers to resolve to use their class time wisely. Time spent in Bible classes is too precious to waste on unrevealed questions.

"If anyone speaks, let him speak as the oracles of God" (1 Pet 4.11).

The Church's Purpose

What is the purpose of the Lord's church? Is it to eradicate poverty, disease, social injustice, and illiteracy from among men? Is it to bring about a cessation of war and conflict? Is it to campaign for a temptation-free society for Christians to live in?

If the church had as one of its great goals the eradication of **disease**, the Lord could have easily equipped it to accomplish that goal. Could not the same power that enabled one blind man to see have enabled all blind men to see; that enabled one lame man to walk have enabled all lame people to walk; that cured many people of varied diseases have cured all people of all diseases? And could not this same power have been given to the church in all generations?

If the church had as one of its great goals the eradication of **poverty**, the Lord could have easily equipped it to accomplish this purpose. After all, He fed the five thousand with five loaves and two fishes. He similarly fed four thousand on another occasion. Could not He who did these marvelous works have enabled His church in all generations to feed, clothe, and shelter the impoverished masses of the world through miraculous powers?

If the Lord had wanted His church to become a lobbyist group to apply political pressure toward a **temptation and persecution-free society** in which to live, He would have given instructions in that direction. He did not even lead His church into a direct effort to destroy **slavery**, but taught the Christian slave to be a better slave and the Christian master to treat his slaves as he would have his heavenly Master treat him (Col 3.22-4.1).

The church's purpose is to save souls and prepare people for eternity. It holds out to the impoverished the hope of some day walking a street of gold, to the suffering a time when there will be no pain, to the sorrowing a moment when "God shall wipe away all tears from their eyes." It tells the tempted and persecuted that there is value in these afflictions that the testing of their faith is more precious than gold, and to rejoice. It tells all to live godly lives in whatever environment they find themselves. It seeks to change people through the power of the gospel, not society through the coercion of legislators. Its weapons "are not carnal but mighty in God." Its motivating theme: "For what will it profit a man, if he gains the whole world, and loses his own soul?"

When churches become involved in hospital and health clinic work, or when they build schools for the education of their children, or when they see as one of their great missions to provide for the world's poverty, or when they feel obligated to create social upheaval and campaign for human rights, or when they feel called upon to express their views on the government's use of nuclear armaments or whatever, they have a distorted view of the purpose of the church.

No Fleshly Incentives

The use of fleshly incentives to draw people to worship services is becoming more and more common. One church offers free cokes, doughnuts, and balloons to its bus riders. Another offers a prize to the child who brings the most visitors. Still another uses some sports figure or entertainer to attract a crowd. Dinners and socials; elaborate church buildings; "Friendliest church in town" or "Fastest-growing church in town" advertising; the list of gimmicks is almost endless.

A study of 1 Corinthians, chapters 1 and 2, suggests that the people of our generation are not the first to demand fleshly incentives. The Jews and Greeks of Paul's day demanded them. "For Jews request a sign and Greeks seek after wisdom" (1 Cor 1.22). Paul could have produced both, but he refused to do so: "But we preach Christ crucified, to the Jews a stumbling block and to the Greeks foolishness, but to those who are called, both Jews and Greeks, Christ the power of God and the wisdom of God"(1.23-24).

Paul recognized the fact that some people are just not "convertible:" "For you see your calling, brethren, that not many wise according to the flesh, not many mighty, not many noble, are called" (1.26). Why are such infrequently called? Because the majority place their trust in the flesh rather than in God. They are fleshly-minded. And Paul was not about to coax fleshly-minded, "unconvertible" people "into the church" by the use of signs, wisdom, excellence of speech, enticing words, or any other fleshly incentive. To do so would result in getting their names on a "church roll," but not in bringing them to Christ to the saving of their souls.

If Paul refused to use signs and wisdom as fleshly incentives, what would have been his reaction to the use of cokes and doughnuts? If he came "not with excellence of speech or of wisdom" (1 Cor 2.1), what would he have said concerning attempts to attract crowds through the use of sports figures and entertainers? If Paul, led by the Holy Spirit, followed a "no fleshly incentive" policy, should that not be our policy? And should we not always be able to say with Paul, "For I determined not to know anything among you except Jesus Christ and Him crucified" (2:2)?

Local Elders or Institutional Board

Considerable controversy has existed over church support of orphan homes. Many contend that there is no New Testament authority for such (this writer is among that number), while others defend the practice. In this article we raise several questions related to the controversy, hoping to clarify the real issue.

What type of orphan homes do you have reference to? We are writing concerning orphan homes which are under institutional boards, such as Child Haven and Tennessee Orphan Home. These boards constitute central agencies soliciting, collecting, and distributing funds from churches of Christ and providing oversight for those churches in the particular work to be done. There is no New Testament authority for such central agencies among churches of Christ. The New Testament knows nothing of inter-church organizations.

Does not James 1.27 authorize church support of such boards for the caring of widows and orphans? James 1.27 says, "Pure and undefiled religion before God and the Father is this: to visit orphans and widows in their trouble, and to keep oneself unspotted from the world." We appreciate the teaching of James 1.27 and try to practice it. No man can go to heaven that does not practice pure and undefiled religion as defined in this passage. But we cannot see authority in the passage for **church** support of **institutional boards** when neither is mentioned in the passage. In fact, a careful reading of this verse along with the verse preceding it will convince the reader that a man's religion is under consideration rather than church action.

Are you saying that there is a distinction to be made between individual responsibility in the Lord's work and local church responsibility? Truly. This distinction is made clearly in 1 Timothy 5.16: "If any believing man or woman (an individual Christian— BH) has widows, let them relieve them, and do not let the church be burdened, that it may relieve those who are really widows." Here is something that the individual is to do that the church is not to do.

The church does have a benevolent responsibility, doesn't it? Yes. The verse just quoted states one of the church's benevolent responsibilities that of relieving widows indeed. Other passages which teach concerning the church's responsibilities in benevolence are Acts 2.44-45; 4.34-35; 6.1-6; Romans 15.25-33; 1 Corinthians 16.1-4; and 2 Corinthians 8-9. We recommend that these passages and any other passages dealing with church action in this field be carefully considered.

But doesn't "benevolence" imply a home for the care of the needy? It may or it may not, but we would not object to the church's providing facilities or food or clothing or supervision if these were needed in fulfilling its benevolent responsibilities. You see, the real question is not whether churches can provide these things, but whether churches can surrender funds and oversight to a central board which in turn must provide these things. The institutional board, or to put it another way, the inter-church organization, is the thing under question. The New Testament does not authorize these central agencies.

Didn't New Testament churches engage in benevolent work? Yes, but each church did its benevolent work through its own organizational framework. When the task of serving tables became too great for the apostles (Acts 6.1-6), they did not suggest the appointment of an institutional board outside the framework of the local church, which in turn could serve in the future as an inter-church organization for all the churches that would later be established. Rather the church was told to "seek out from **among you** seven,,,whom we may appoint over this business." We are simply saying that each church should do its own benevolent work under the oversight of its own elders assisted by its own deacons. This is the Bible plan.

Suppose conditions arise making it impossible for the congregation to provide for its own needy? Such conditions did arise in the New Testament (Acts 11.27-30; Rom 15.25-26). In those cases, churches that were able sent to the needy churches, enabling those needy churches to provide for their own. But the reader would do well to observe that the funds were not sent to an institutional board, but to the elders of the needy churches (Acts 11.27-30).

In summary, we encourage every Christian to practice "pure and undefiled religion" to the extent of his ability. We encourage churches to provide for their own needy under the oversight of their own elders. And, we encourage Christians everywhere to think again about the central agencies that have been created among churches of Christ. "And whatever you do in word or deed, do all in the name of the Lord Jesus..." (Col 3.17).

The Gospel Is for All

The church that pleases God will reach out to all classes of men: to the poor, the unfortunate, the depraved, to all who need salvation through Christ's blood. It does not limit its influence to people who are socially and economically compatible. The gospel is for all.

Jesus taught this lesson both in word and action. He showed as much concern for an immoral Samaritan woman as He did for a rich young ruler; as much concern for a publican named Zacchaeus as He did for a Pharisee named Simon. His closest followers were from the poorer classes of society. Yet there were rich men who were influenced by Him, too. He sought to bring all men to Himself. And when He commissioned His apostles, He said, "Go into all the world and preach the gospel to every creature…" (Mark 16.15).

Christians do not find common ground in their social and economic standings, but in their mutual love for the Lord, in their common faith, and in their shared hope of eternal life. When people truly love the Lord, distinctions of a worldly nature fade into nothingness. The rich man rejoices "in his humiliation," while the brother of low degree rejoices "in his exaltation"—the two reaching equality in Christ (Jas 1.9-10). If one cannot find room in his heart for people of all classes, there is something seriously lacking in his faith and devotion to the Lord.

The early church learned this lesson well. They preached to the poor as well as to the rich; to the lowly as well as to governors. Their converts included even the Samaritans and the Gentiles. The grossly immoral were changed by the gospel. And when some discourtesy was shown to the poor or the outcasts, stern rebukes were administered (Gal 2.11-14; Jas 2.1-9).

Is there someone reading this article who feels "down and out," who is sure no one cares for him because he is so poor, or has been so immoral, or is handicapped, or friendless? If you are that one, let me assure you that the Lord cares for you; and there are people who care about you, too. The gospel is for you.

Is there someone reading this article who is embarrassed when some obviously poor individual, or someone of immoral reputation, or someone in unfortunate circumstances enters the worship assembly? If you are that one, you need to repent. With that kind of attitude, you would have felt very uncomfortable in the presence of the Lord while He was upon the earth.

The church is to be made up of holy and godly people who strive to be like their Master. But the church reaches out to godless people of all classes in the hope that they can be transformed in Christ's image and be saved eternally. "Christ Jesus came into the world to save sinners..." (1 Tim 1.15).

Attitudes Toward the Weak

The Messiah's attitude toward the spiritually weak is pictured by Isaiah in the following words: "A bruised reed He will not break, and smoking flax He will not quench" (Isa 42.3).

In our zeal for purity and strength in the church we may be guilty of doing the very thing that our Lord does not want done. We create a mental image of what the ideal church ought to be, and then go about to establish one. Every member is going to attend every service. Every member will be "sound" in his convictions. Worldliness will not be tolerated. This church is not going to have the weaknesses that characterize other churches we know of. This is going to be a strong church, a model church.

A new convert is made, and immediately he is indoctrinated in what this church is, and the contribution he is expected to make to the maintaining of this ideal.

Each newcomer is viewed as a potential threat. If he's not going to "line up" we don't want him. Weaker members are handled with a "shape up or ship out" attitude. People soon recognize that there is far more concern for the image of the church as an organization than for them as struggling and weak children of God. While the Messiah is tenderly and delicately nursing these "bruised reeds" back to health, we may be there crushing them. While He cups His hands around these fluttering, dimly-burning flames to protect what fire is left, we may be there quenching them.

We are not suggesting that unrepentant false teachers and immoral members ought to be tolerated. They must be warned, marked, and withdrawn from. Nor are we suggesting that the weak ought to be left alone in their weakness. They must be taught, encouraged, reproved, rebuked, and exhorted, but with all longsuffering, and with a view toward strengthening them. "Warn those who are unruly, comfort the fainthearted, uphold the weak, be patient with all" (1 Thes 5.14). Ask not what they can do for the church, but what the church can do for them.

As long as there is a little life in that "bruised reed," there is hope. Don't crush it! As long as there is a little fire left, it might be fanned to burn more brightly. Don't extinguish it!

Reinstated?

We are hearing some rather strange expressions these days. A man was telling us recently that he had gone forward the Sunday before to be "reinstated." A woman said she was thinking of "going back into the church." Are such expressions a problem in terminology? Or are we faced with a problem in concept? Are people thinking of the church as an organization similar to the P.T.A., in and out of which they can go at will, returning simply to be "reinstated"?

Unfaithfulness is not just a matter of dropping out of the church for a while. It is a matter of trampling "the Son of God underfoot," of insulting "the Spirit of grace," of giving "occasion to the enemies of the LORD to blaspheme," of turning one's back on the Lord and His promises, of living in sin and flirting with eternal damnation. Imagine a person's being in such a position, and then coming forward to be "reinstated"!!! What that person needs to do is repent, fall on his knees before God, and confess to Him and to his brethren, "I have sinned," and cry to God for mercy.

We are not questioning God's mercy. He is prepared to forgive His wayward child; to run to him, fall on his neck, and kiss him, to place the best robe on his back, a ring on his finger, shoes on his feet, to kill the fatted calf and be merry. But this abundant forgiveness is for that wayward child who returns with a full recognition of his sin and unworthiness, who confesses his sins, who asks, not to be "reinstated" as a son, but to be received back only as a hired servant. Forgiveness is for the penitent.

May the Lord help us to see sin in its true ugliness, to "abhor what is evil" and "cling to what is good," to remember the price paid by our Lord for our forgiveness, to be faithful, and to humbly acknowledge our sins when we do fall. And when we are forgiven, let us not speak glibly of "going back into the church," but let us speak of the grace of God that could save "a wretch like me."

"Blessed are those who mourn, for **they** shall be comforted" (Matt 5.4).

Good Leadership

What are the characteristics of good leadership? Good leadership has vision to see what needs to be done. Good leadership moves forward, is positive in its approach, stirs confidence in others, and convinces them that the impossible task can be accomplished.

Good leadership has faith in people. Good leadership believes that others want to work and that they will respond when properly challenged; it places the best possible construction on the actions of others. Good leadership "bears all things, believes all things, hopes all things, endures all things," because good leadership loves.

Good leadership does not run ahead of others. It does not do everything itself. In fact, it frequently steps aside and waits—sometimes anxiously—while others are given a chance to perform the tasks which they are capable of performing. Good leadership is not nearly so concerned with getting **things** done as it is with developing **people** into useful, mature servants of the Lord. Good leadership is constantly producing leadership in others.

Good leadership has a real concern for others and has the ability to communicate that concern. Good leadership is patient, understanding; it is neither too quick to rebuke nor is it indulgent toward sin. Good leadership places itself in the other man's position to see things from his viewpoint.

Good leadership is humble, is willing to acknowledge mistakes; it can accept criticism and separate the constructive from the destructive. Good leadership seeks the praise of God rather than the praise of men; it sacrifices popularity to do God's will.

Good leadership has conviction, but is not stubborn or headstrong. It listens to others and views their ideas objectively. Good leadership treats all alike; it is impartial. Good leadership is frank and candid, but is kind.

Good leadership is self-confident, but not proud; it does not have to be self-promoting.

The church needs men and women who are leaders, but what a difference between those who **seek** to lead and those who **truly** lead.

The Cost of Influence and Reputation

There are people in this world who are possessed with natural ability to lead and command respect of others. Call it charm, charisma, magnetism, or whatever, such people wield a powerful influence on those who look up to them as the embodiment of all they would like to become themselves.

Peter apparently possessed such qualities among the apostles; and there were David, Deborah, Nehemiah, and others. We have known such people in our day and have been influenced by them. Each reader can probably think of some "hero" of faith that he or she has looked up to through the years.

The opportunities for good that such people possess are tremendous; **but so are the responsibilities**. It is true that sin is sin, whoever commits it; that sin will separate one from God just as quickly as it will another. But the adverse consequences of one's sins increase dramatically with the increase of the influence and reputation he enjoys among others. The confidence of others is a trust that must be carefully protected. Once that trust is in place, the person to whom it is committed has responsibilities that others of more normal influence and reputation do not have; and the more people involved in the trust, the greater the responsibility.

Those of reputation must be prepared for greater public scandal when they sin. Nathan told David that because of his adultery he had "given great occasion to the enemies of the Lord to blaspheme" (2 Sam 12.14). Others had committed adultery in Israel, and their adultery had gone unnoticed by the enemies of God. But this was David! It was inevitable that the sin of this one man of influence and reputation would result in greater scandal than the sins of a multitude of people of lesser influence and reputation.

Those of reputation must be prepared for sterner rebuke when they sin than those of lesser reputation. Paul speaks of withstanding Peter "to his face" when Peter withdrew from eating with the

Gentiles (Gal 2.11-14). Paul's rebuke of Peter was "before them all." Peter was hardly the first Jewish Christian to refuse to eat with Gentile Christians, but Paul obviously recognized the seriousness of Peter's actions because of his greater reputation and influence. Others were following his lead on this occasion, including Barnabas. Peter could not enjoy the luxury of a private meeting with Paul; Peter had to face the sting of immediate and open rebuke. Peter had betrayed a trust. Nothing less than open rebuke could counteract the harm that was resulting. Sterner rebuke is simply a cost—an inevitable cost—of influence and reputation.

Those of reputation must live more cautiously than others if they would maintain their influence and good name. Every Christian is warned not to place a stumbling block in his brother's way (Rom 14.13; 1 Cor 8.9), but one who is known and admired by thousands of brethren in many places obviously will have to be more cautious than one who is known and admired by only a few brethren locally. Paul would have to give up far more to be "all things to all men" than would some Christian who had never been outside his home community. That's just the cost of influence and reputation. If one is not willing to pay that cost if he is determined to be unbending in his conduct "no matter what others might think"—he needs to come to a greater appreciation of the value of a good name (Prov 22.1).

Those of reputation must be especially careful to build upon Jesus Christ, the true foundation, rather than upon themselves. The words, "For we do not preach ourselves, but Christ Jesus the Lord," must become their motto (2 Cor 4.5). Those who place their loyalty in men of name and reputation are in error. Their faith is not what it ought to be. But those who deliberately use charisma and flattery to attract a following are also in error (1 Thes 2.1-13). The more natural charisma one is blessed (?) with, the more cautious he must be.

When "Shoeless" Joe Jackson, a star Chicago White Sox outfielder, was involved in the "Blackstocking" scandal of the 1920s and was on his way to trial, a small boy, hurt, disappointed, with tears in his eyes, was heard to cry, "Say it ain't so, Joe, say it ain't so." Each reader is likely somebody's hero. Other readers are men and women of widespread influence. Let each one, when he is tempted, and **before he yields**, look ahead to the tears, and hurt and disillusionment that he is about to bring to those who look up to him; let him hear their potential cries of "Say it ain't so, Joe;" and, motivated by their confidence and his own love for the Lord, let him "resist the devil." For, if he betrays the trust that has been committed to him, he can be saved eternally through repentance and forgiveness—for this we are so grateful!—but he likely will never recover the confidence he has lost. Right or wrong, that's reality. It is the cost—the inevitable cost—of influence and reputation.

We Believe, And Therefore Speak

The preaching of the apostles proceeded from hearts full of conviction. They had observed the miracles of Jesus; they had heard His teaching; three of them had been with Him in the mount, and had heard those words spoken from heaven, "This is My beloved Son, in whom I am well pleased. Hear Him;" they had seen His composure as He was arrested in the garden; they had carefully examined evidences of His resurrection, and had talked with Him, eaten with Him, felt of Him; they had watched as He ascended until a cloud received Him out of their sight. They believed! And so full were they of faith that their faith overflowed in words. They could not hold back that message which burned in their hearts.

They preached it everywhere: in the synagogues and in the temple, in the streets and from house to house, in governors' mansions and in prisons, in market places and from Mars Hill, on ships and in chariots, in upper rooms and on riverbanks.

They preached it to the rich and to the poor, to worshipers of God and to worshipers of idols, to the humble and to the proud, to the lowly and to the mighty, to the educated and to the uneducated, to the good and to the bad, to the moral and to the immoral.

They preached it to drunkards, to adulterers, to homosexuals, to idolaters, to sorcerers, to kings, to governmental officials, to army officers, to jailers, to ship captains, to beggars. They preached it and preached it and preached it!

Because they preached it they were imprisoned, beaten, scourged, stoned, mocked, ridiculed, threatened; they were victims of lies, deceit, conspiracy, uproars, mob violence, shipwreck, ambush; they lived in poverty, often hungering, and with "no certain dwelling place"; but nothing could stop them from preaching as long as they had breath. They believed, and their faith forced them to preach regardless of the consequences. They believed, and therefore spoke (2 Cor 4.3).

What did they preach? They preached that message revealed to them by the Holy Spirit, God's divine message (1 Cor 2.6-13). They had no time for opinions, human philosophies, or politics, nor was their faith centered upon such things. The message that burned in their hearts was a message concerning the Christ and salvation through Him. They believed in Christ, in the efficacy of His blood, and in the power of His gospel. They believed, and therefore they spoke that message and that message only.

Faith! In that one word may lay the most important element of effective evangelism. When we come to believe as did those apostles, when we become so full of faith that we can hardly restrain ourselves, when the message of salvation burns within us as it did in them, we will be teaching others and we will be doing so effectively. Until then our words may contain an unmistakable emptiness that will render them powerless in changing the hearts of men.

Holding Forth the Word of Life

Hello, Simon, did you hear about the incident up at the temple yesterday? We were a little late for the hour of prayer, and when we got there, we heard this awful commotion in Solomon's porch. Peter and John had just healed a lame man—they're always trying to get attention, you know—and Peter was doing the preaching as usual.

Well, Simon, you should have heard the sermon. No, on second thought, I'm glad you were spared the agony. Do you know that Peter preached the same old sermon that he used on Pentecost? People get tired of hearing the same old thing. And he was so offensive. He actually accused them of being ignorant and said they had been guilty in the crucifixion of Jesus. They were guilty, of course, but Peter doesn't have to be so plainspoken right to their face. And scripture, scripture, scripture! I get so tired of hearing scripture all the time. I thought he would never get through. And, would you believe, it was the very time I had chosen to take Joseph with me. I was just mortified! I apologized for what happened, but I just know he'll never go with me again. In fact, he might never speak to me again.

But that's not all! Before Peter got through preaching, the priest and the captain of the temple and the Sadducees came up and arrested Peter and John right there. Simon, I was so embarrassed! We'll never do any good with all this bad publicity. They get a good crowd together and then ruin it all by getting arrested. The apostles don't know a thing about gaining public favor.

And all they want is money. They probably want more people to sell their possessions. They won't get mine! I can't stand fanatics; besides, those people are just showing off giving all that money. And, by the way, Simon, I hear they are counting the number of converts again. Boy, they sure do go for numbers. But let them count. The way they're going, there won't be a church left around here. We can just get ready to close the doors. Nobody wants to be a part of a church where the preachers preach the same old thing all the time and are constantly being arrested.

Did you say something, Simon? What did you say? The number is what? The number of men is up to…to…5,000?

If You Are Planning to Preach

If you are planning to preach, give careful attention to the following three basic elements of successful preaching.

1. **Spirituality**. The faithful preacher has a deep devotion to God and His word. He prays often. He lives with a constant awareness of God's nearness; he "walks with God." His character is beyond reproach. He hates sin and error, but loves truth and righteousness. "His delight is in the law of the LORD, and in His law he meditates day and night." If you want to preach, but lack these qualities, then

wait. Develop these first. You can hardly motivate others to become what you have not become yourself.

2. **Preparation**. Learn to **read**. Reading comprehension is an essential tool to understanding the scriptures and related books. Learn to **think**. Many of the things you will read in commentaries and even in brotherhood periodicals will be false. Woe is that man who in his preaching and Bible class teaching merely parrots what he has read. Learn to **differentiate**: between truth and error, between fact and supposition, between what is clearly taught and what is in the "gray" area, between what is congregationally applicable and what is individually applicable, between the time to "rock the boat" and the time not to "rock the boat." "Be wise as serpents and harmless as doves" (Matt 10.16). Learn **courage**. You will be faced with pressures and intimidation from every side. To some, you will preach too hard; to some, too soft. Some will pressure you to compromise; others will try to force you into some "hard-line" position which you really can't find in the scriptures. Please God. Get along with the brethren as far as possible, but not at the risk of losing your soul. If problems do develop, take a long, hard look at "self." We fear that many a man has created a "doctrinal" crisis in an effort to cover up his own bad disposition and dictatorial attitude.

3. **Presentation**. You are no longer a schoolboy playing a part on a stage. Neither are you a comedian being paid to entertain an audience. You are a dying man preaching to dying men and women the only message on earth that can save their souls. Speak to **them**. Help them to see their sins, and point them to the Savior. Speak with the warmth, and love, and sincerity that will let them know that you care for them and their eternal destiny. What you speak may be more important, but how you speak is important, too.

L.A. Mott, Jr. (*Notebook on Jeremiah*, p. 67) writes: "Someone has said that there are three kinds of preachers. The first has to say something—he is a paid talker who has to fill a certain amount of time each week. The second has something to say, and that is a whole lot better. But best of all is the third—the man who has something to say **and has to say it**. That is the kind of preacher Jeremiah was." And that's the kind of preacher you must be.

Get Me a Job Preaching

We have been asked to write concerning the danger of professionalism among preachers, a danger of which many are totally unaware.

We must preface our warnings with a grateful acknowledgment that there are many faithful and dedicated men throughout the world who have devoted their lives to preaching. Many of these are young men whose spirituality, love for truth, and concern for souls have compelled them to share the gospel with others. They are willing to go where they are needed rather than to the places where salary and prestige are the greatest. They see preaching as a service to be rendered in a spirit of sacrifice and unselfishness. There is plenty of room in God's kingdom for such men.

But preaching can also be viewed as a career to be pursued with self-seeking goals and ambition. There was a time when few would have preached because of financial considerations. But times have changed. Preachers' salaries have increased. Churches are clamoring for preachers. Opportunities are there, while employment in other fields is difficult to find. In fact, there are probably few jobs where a young man can begin at a higher salary than in preaching, and especially if he chooses to push the church for every penny "he can get out of them." Besides, there are no educational or job training requirements. The only requirements in some cases are a smattering of Bible knowledge, a good personality, and a gift of gab. Add to this the glamour of standing before audiences and being "looked up to," and obviously the temptation can be great for a young man who can't find a job otherwise to decide to preach.

Such men may accomplish some good if they indeed preach Christ, and we shall rejoice in that good (Phil 1.12-18). But they themselves are so vulnerable to the temptation to compromise, to flatter, to "water down" their teaching (or toughen it in some cases), or, in short, to do whatever is necessary to enhance their position and "advance" their career. They are also "sitting ducks" for disillusionment. They have begun preaching for the wrong reasons, and their mistake endangers both their own souls and the welfare of the Lord's church.

To all who preach or who are thinking of preaching, we would suggest: if, like Jeremiah, you find God's word in your heart as a burning fire, and you cannot stay silent; if, like Paul, you feel a driving compulsion to preach the gospel; if, like the apostles, you cannot but speak the things which they saw and heard; if, like Timothy, you have genuine concern for the state of others; if you would preach, whether supported or not supported, whether in season or out of season, whether "looked up to" by the church or persecuted by the church; if you would preach, as did all first-century preachers, even under the threat of death, then by all means preach, and receive and be grateful for whatever moral and financial support the churches give you. But, if otherwise, for your sake and the gospel's, find some other means of making a living.

Balanced Preaching

The faithful preacher preaches a message of hope and grace, while at the same time repudiating a spirit of complacency and carelessness. He holds before others a God who is both good and severe.

A lady once said to a preacher, "_____, the best thing you could do for people when you baptize them is to leave them under just a little while longer." Her statement manifests a belief that the way to heaven is so difficult that there is little chance that even the most sincere can get there. Such an attitude is dangerous, indeed. It would cause a Christian to stumble over the first obstacle thrown in his way. "Why should I struggle?" would be his obvious question, "I'm probably not going to make it to heaven anyway."

A faithful preacher does not want to foster such a pessimistic and fatalistic attitude by his preaching. He wants to preach a gospel of hope and assurance. He wants to convince people that they can go to heaven if they so determine, that their "labor is not in vain in the Lord," that they can "make (their) calling and election sure," and can take definite steps to ensure that abundant entrance "into the everlasting kingdom of our Lord and Savior Jesus Christ," that they can "die in the Lord" and can even "have boldness in the day of judgment." He wants his hearers to know that they serve a

God who "is merciful and gracious, slow to anger, and abounding in mercy," who "pities those who fear Him" as "a father pities his children," who "knows our name" and "remembers that we are dust" (Psa 103.8-14). If he succeeds, he offers his hearers great incentives to faithfulness. Convince people that they really are going to heaven, and they will suffer ridicule, deprivation, imprisonment, and even death in order to get there.

At the same time, a faithful preacher does not want to foster a complacent and careless attitude. God's grace must not be viewed as a license to sin. "Diligence," "sincerity," "abound," "faith": these are key words in the scriptures. The abundant entrance into the everlasting kingdom is for those who diligently supply in their faith the "Christian graces" and abound in them (2 Pet 1.5-11). God's forgiveness is for those who "walk in the light" and "confess [their sins]" (1 John 1.6-10). Such must be the continuous conduct of a Christian if he wants to live in continuous hope and assurance.

A faithful preacher seeks for careful balance in these matters. We fear that current questions concerning God's grace are driving men to opposite poles, some almost exclusively preaching God's severity; others almost exclusively preaching His goodness. Every man must examine himself and his own teaching. Let each preach so as to bring others to say, "You make me glad I'm a Christian; you help me to see my faults; you motivate me to try harder." What a contrast between this response and the one at the beginning of the article! Which response would most likely result from **your** preaching?

Scholarly, but Practical

The preaching of Christ and His apostles was scholarly, but practical. Scholarship was with them a means to an end, never an end in itself. Their goal in preaching was to change men, to "present every man perfect in Christ Jesus" (Col 1.28).

True scholarship among faithful preachers will tend to conceal itself. It will be hidden behind the cross of Christ and the preacher's own love for the souls of men. The true scholar does not have to call attention to himself. The true Christian will not do so.

No more scholarly work was ever written than the book of Romans. That book, however, is no mere irrelevant discussion of difficult passages that would impress the world with its scholarship. It is practical throughout, as Paul persuades men to seek for salvation, not through a system of law, but through faith in Jesus Christ.

Who would question the Lord's scholarship in His sermon on the mount? The beauty in that sermon, though, is to be found in its simplicity, its applicability, its straightforwardness, its challenge to the consciences of men. These are qualities that have endeared it to its readers and wrought changes in the lives of millions of people.

The Bible abounds in examples of powerful preaching: Moses' "Let My people go," Joshua's "Choose…this day whom you will serve," Nathan's "You are the man," Elijah's "How long will you falter between two opinions?" Daniel's "You have been weighed in the balances, and found wanting," John's "It is not lawful for you to have her," Peter's "God has made this Jesus, whom you crucified, both Lord and Christ." Those who heard these preachers may not have raved of their scholarship, but they understood what they said and were never really the same after having heard them.

We do not mean to discourage scholarship; we rather encourage it. No man should preach who has not sought diligently to "handle aright the word of truth." But when one enters the pulpit, it's time to "reprove, rebuke, exhort" rather than to display brilliance. Scholarly, but practical preaching has always been the need, and it remains the need for today.

Those Additional Points

"I thought of a point that would fit nicely into that sermon," the good brother says as he shakes hands with the preacher. Of course the preacher has already thought of numbers of ways he could improve the same sermon and may be feeling discouraged over his efforts. But he might do well to remember that such additional thoughts coming from his audience are not as a rule indicative of poor preaching, but of good preaching.

Good preaching does not cater to people who, like little birds, sit with their mouths open ready to swallow anything that is fed them. Good preaching challenges an audience to think and evaluate. Good preaching plants seeds of thought that can germinate and grow. Good preaching in time familiarizes people with scripture, scripture which they are likely to recall when applicable points are discussed. It should not be surprising when those thinking people want to share their thoughts with their teacher at the conclusion of a lesson. And when they come up with true gems (How often it can happen!) that can contribute greatly to sermons, it may just be a strong indication that the teaching program of that congregation is working with rare efficiency.

Further, good preaching begins with a purpose and drives toward a conclusion. Material that contributes to that purpose is retained; material—even good material— that does not contribute is culled. Good preaching does not have as its goal to exhaust a subject (or an audience), but to prick the hearts of hearers and bring them to desired conclusions. Good preaching often accomplishes its purposes with a few, carefully selected passages, developed fully, rather than with rapid-fire quotation of every passage that can be recalled on the subject. It is not surprising, consequently, when the audience is reminded of scriptures and thoughts that are not included in the sermon. Such is to be desired.

Good preaching focuses attention on the Christ rather than on the speaker. Good preaching is "Acts 2" type of preaching. Is not the purpose of Peter's sermon obvious as he drives to the conclusion "that God has made this Jesus, whom you crucified, both Lord and Christ"? Could not all of us think of other applicable Old Testament passages than the three that Peter used? And could not a greater discussion have taken place on such themes as "Hades" and "God's foreknowledge"? There is no doubt that Peter's sermon included more than is recorded in Acts 2 (verse 40 says so), but what the Holy Spirit records for us is a sermon with a definite purpose driving toward a logical conclusion supported by scripture and discussion all of which contribute to that purpose. This is good preaching for it is Holy Spirit inspired preaching.

We fall short of the ideal. But we can improve, and the best gauge of improvement may well be the additional comments that proceed from a challenged audience.

Understanding a Preacher's Needs

How much should a preacher be paid? He should receive enough support that, **with reasonable management,** he can live free of major financial worries. This will vary considerably, depending upon the number of children a man may have, the amount of sickness suffered in the family, his responsibility toward needy relatives, etc. But no preacher can do an effective work if he is constantly troubled by financial worries.

Churches should understand the extra expenses incurred by a preacher. He will have to spend more money for clothing and gasoline than the average member of the average church. He will entertain guests more frequently. He must keep a good car in good mechanical condition, for he is often called out of town for funerals and other needs. He uses his own private car every day in the Lord's work.

Preachers enjoy few fringe benefits. There are some. Other Christians often share the produce of their gardens, pass on the clothing their children have outgrown, and show kindnesses in many other ways. These thoughtful gestures are not to be minimized. Occasionally a businessman will render some special favor to preachers. Meetings usually result in additional support for those who are asked to preach in them. But a preacher usually arranges for his own hospitalization insurance and retirement plan (if he has one). These involve a heavy expense. He pays Social Security taxes as a self-employed person. These facts should be considered by churches.

We sometimes hear of gross unfairness to preachers. We have heard of churches deliberately "starving" their preachers into moving. What a cowardly way of handling a matter. Other churches pay a preacher well, but some of the members begrudge every penny he receives and make sure he is aware of their displeasure.

We encourage churches to appreciate good men who preach the gospel faithfully, be thoughtful of their financial needs, and support them cheerfully. We encourage preachers to be thankful for the thoughtfulness of good churches. Let's not let poor relationships between churches and preachers hinder the performance of the great task God has placed before us.

Society's Lowest Class

What class of people constitutes the lowest element of society? The drug pushers? Pornographers? Child abusers? Freeloaders?

According to Isaiah it's none of these: "Therefore the Lord will cut off head and tail from Israel ("from the highest to the lowest," we would say—BH), "palm branch and bulrush in one day" (Isa 9.14). Then in the next verse he identifies "the tail," the lowest of the people: "The elder and honorable, he is the head; the prophet who teaches lies, he is the tail."

There is no lower element of society than false teachers. They claim to be guides to heaven, but they point the way to hell. Their victims are not those who seek wickedness; they are those who seek salvation. The spiritually blind come to them for guidance, only to be led over a precipice. The spiritually sick come for healing, only to be given poison. The lost come for soul-saving truth, only to be given soul-damning error.

True teachers of the word suffer because of them. They approach the lost with the pure gospel, only to find them already "turned off" from religion because of false teachers. Then when they do find the earnest seeker, their two or three hours per week with him are counteracted by hours and hours of exposure to the false promises, dramatic testimonials, and deceitful tactics of the present-day television evangelists. The final product is not a convert to the Lord, but a disillusioned victim who is prepared to condemn all religion as hypocrisy and fraud. No wonder Isaiah brands them as the lowest of the low.

Some are intentional deceivers while others are unintentional. The intentional deceivers are motivated by greed, selfish ambition, and, in some cases, sensuality (2 Pet 2.1-3). They make merchandise of their victims. They beg money, grieving over their "dire straits," when in reality they have huge amounts of money invested in stocks and bonds. They claim to be lovers of God when in reality they are lovers of self. On the outside they appear to be "angels of light," but on the inside they are "false apostles" and "deceitful workers" (2 Cor 11.13-15).

Others are false teachers unintentionally. They themselves are victims of deceit, and they go out deceiving others. They do so thinking they are rendering service to God (John 16.2). They are sincere, but they are also guilty, guilty of leading others to hell. For this very reason James wrote: "My brethren, let not many of you become teachers, knowing that we shall receive a stricter judgment" (Jas 3.1). The warning is clear: eagerness to share the gospel with others is admirable, but woe to that man who rushes into the work without due consideration of the responsibilities and judgment that go with it.

False teachers are not good people. They are the lowest element of society. What a fearful thing if I am one—or am deceived by one—or lend support to one!

Caution—Corruption Ahead

Reports of sin and corruption among religious leaders are on the increase. We read of preachers who beg constantly for money, often receiving generous donations representing great sacrifice from the poor, while they themselves bask in luxury and huge financial surpluses. We hear of adultery and theft, lying and gambling, and in many cases the religious leaders are guilty. Then insult is added to injury when we read "Reverend" before their names. What a terrible day it will be when such men stand before the Lord in judgment!

While we are saddened by the misconduct itself, we are even more saddened by the fact that such misconduct causes many people to lose confidence in all religion. They turn their back on Christ, His word, and His church. They assume that everyone who claims to be a Christian is just like the corrupt religious leaders they have heard of. They assume there is no real value in Christianity. This constitutes a terrible loss to everyone concerned.

We make the following observations for your consideration:

1. Not all religion and religious leaders are corrupt. There are godly, dedicated, conscientious servants of Jesus Christ in your community and throughout the world. They don't make the headlines. They go about their work quietly and without fanfare. But they are there and you need to be aware of their presence and example. Look for them. They may even be among your acquaintances.

2. Wickedness on the part of leaders in religion does not prove that the religion itself is false. The misconduct of one of Jesus' apostles (Judas) was no proof that Jesus Himself was corrupt or that His religion was vain. In the same way, misconduct on the part of some of His professed followers today is no proof that His religion is corrupt and vain.

3. If you allow the misconduct of some leader in religion to turn you away from the Lord and be lost eternally, you are a loser along with him. Your pointing the finger of blame at him will not make your eternal suffering any easier to bear.

4. Your faith must be in Jesus Christ, not in some man. Your loyalty must be to Christ. A man, even a good man, can let you down, but Jesus Christ will never let you

down. He will never leave you nor forsake you as long as you maintain faithfulness and loyalty to Him.

5. You can go to heaven whatever others choose to do. While faithful service to the Lord brings us into fellowship with others in His church, faithfulness itself is an individual matter. You will stand before the Lord in judgment alone. You can go to heaven even if all others of your generation forsake Christ. Think about it. The question you must ponder is not where some religious leader will spend eternity, but where **you** will spend eternity. May the Lord help us all to rise above the world and its influences to serve Him in sincerity and truth.

If He Has a Soul

A wonderful prospect for conversion is described in the tenth chapter of Acts: "A devout man and one who feared God with all his household, who gave alms generously to the people, and prayed to God always." If this man could just learn the truth he would obey it.

Tremendous pressure, however, was against Peter's preaching to him. He was a Gentile, and the Jews hated the Gentiles. Could Peter preach to one of this hated class of people? What would his brethren say? Would preaching to the Gentiles hurt his influence among the Jews? Maybe Peter shouldn't go. Maybe Cornelius should somehow learn the gospel on his own.

Peter might have followed this very line of reasoning had the Lord allowed it. But through a vision the Lord taught Peter that he "should not call any man common or unclean" (Acts 10.28). Because Peter learned this lesson and courageously preached to Cornelius and his household, the great work among the Gentiles, which has resulted in the salvation of thousands through the ages, was begun.

Are there not hated classes of people in our society? Is it possible that in our search for "prospects" we have limited ourselves to those who are of the same economic, racial, and educational position which we occupy? And is it possible that in so limiting ourselves, we may be overlooking some of the greatest prospects that we have? Do we need to be taught that we are not to call any man common or unclean?

A quote from Henry Ficklin, an aged brother in Eastern Kentucky, now deceased, impressed me recently. Brother Ficklin and another brother were making house calls. Brother Ficklin was a bit uncertain as to the location of one house where they were going, so the other brother, seeing a man in a barn lot, pulled over and asked, "Do you suppose this is the man we are looking for?" "I suppose so," brother Ficklin replied, "if he has a soul he's the man we are looking for."

If he has a soul…. The Hebrew writer said that Jesus tasted "death for everyone" (Heb 2.9). Let us not be guilty because of our prejudices of withholding the gospel from the "Corneliuses" of our society.

They Must See the Need

An acquaintance of mine, hearing recently of a family that had suffered considerable misfortune, went to the home to investigate. He found a father suffering from multiple sclerosis. The mother had just been involved in a serious automobile accident. A son, injured in the accident, was in the hospital. Moved by the misfortunes of the good family, he wrote out a small check, and gave it to the mother. Tears welled up in her eyes as she thanked him and expressed how kind everyone had been. She was so grateful.

The same man went that week to see a young couple who were not Christians. He offered to study the scriptures with them, specifically suggesting the book of Acts. He was trying to give this couple something far greater than a small check. He wanted to bring them to the salvation of their souls, to an eternal home in heaven, to an escape from the fires of hell. The young couple thanked him, but said they were not interested in studying at this time.

Before we criticize the young couple, we need to analyze **why** the difference; viz, the first family recognized their need for what was being offered, while the second didn't. That young couple probably never realized what they were in reality refusing. If they ever awaken to their need, they will accept the gospel with a joy and excitement that will even surpass that of the first family mentioned.

We approach different types of people in our work for the Lord. Some know they are lost and are seeking help. Others do not know they are lost, but are interested in the Bible, and will agree to study the scriptures. They can be brought to understand their lost condition through study. But still others are unconcerned, have no interest in Bible study, and really don't want to be bothered. These require a completely different kind of approach, a great amount of patience, and much prayer. We must not give up on these. In time many can be brought to see their lost condition and repent.

The 3,000 who were baptized on Pentecost had no concern for learning about Jesus when the day began. The same could be said of the jailer of Philippi. Saul's only interest as he started out for Damascus was to imprison and persecute Christians. He would have hardly agreed to a study at that time. The woman of Samaria had little concern for her soul as she went to Jacob's well for water; but oh! the skill with which the Master Teacher brought her to see her sinful condition! Each of these demonstrated a complete change in attitude **as soon as he saw his lost condition.**

This complete change in attitude on the part of so many un-concerned, even belligerent ones of the first century gives us hope for the unconcerned of our age. In fact, maybe someday, with the Lord's help, we can report the obedience of the young couple mentioned above.

Truth's Consequences

The consequences of truth are sometimes bitter. Many a man has lost his job or home, or friends or life because of his stand for truth. Many a preacher has been ousted from the pulpit, having neither house nor salary, because he preached the truth. Many a person has had his name slandered and maligned because of truth. With all such people, love for truth is greater than love for comfort, security, or even life itself.

Unfortunate indeed is the man who looks ahead to evaluate the consequences of a position before evaluating the position itself. Such a man will rarely come to a knowledge of truth. His thoughts concerning "What will my wife think?" or "Where will I preach?" or "Won't I be condemning my good mother to hell?" or "How will I explain my change to good ole Brother Jones?" or "How will I support my family?" or "Everybody will think I'm crazy," may well blind his mind to whatever evidence is at hand. The man who really demonstrates a love for truth is the man who studies every subject objectively and then lets the consequences—whether they are good or bad—take care of themselves.

Unfortunate too is the man who complains and grieves over the consequences of truth, for truth must bring joy to the heart, whatever may be its consequences. Self-pity may lead one to "sell the truth" and to profane this precious commodity. If pity is to be felt, it must be felt for that person who has never suffered the consequences of truth, for such a man has obviously loved the praises of men more than the praises of God.

No men ever felt the consequences of truth to a greater degree than did the apostles, but they faced all such consequences "rejoicing that they were counted worthy to suffer shame for His name" (Acts 5.41). Worthy! There's the key! The man who lets a fear of consequences dictate his position on every question never suffers, for he is not worthy to suffer. Pity him! But the person who stands for truth regardless of the consequences shall suffer, for he is worthy to suffer. Rejoice with him!

What a difference between the man who is "heaven" oriented and that one who is "this world" oriented!

Shallow Thinking—False Conclusions

Superficial thinking often leads to false conclusions. This fact is easily illustrated by the Jews' rejection of Jesus as the Christ. We sometimes marvel at their unbelief, but how could they have accepted Him? After all, Jesus had come from Galilee, and the scriptures had plainly stated that the Christ would come from Bethlehem (John 7.41-42). And if He really were the Christ, why would He encourage people to break the Sabbath (Matt 12.1-13; John 5.1-16), and even fail to keep it Himself (John 9.16)? It was true that Jesus performed great miracles, and His feeding of the five thousand was especially intriguing, but Moses had fed the Israelites with manna, and he never claimed to have come from God (John 6.30-31). And if He really were the Christ, why did He allow sinners to touch Him? Wouldn't He have known what manner of people they were (Luke 7.39)? Besides, His death was obvious proof that He was not the Christ, for the law had said that the Christ would live forever (John 12.34). Now, if He had suddenly come down from the cross, they would have believed in Him (Matt 27.42), but there He was, "stricken, smitten by God, and afflicted" (Isa 53.4). He could not have been Christ!

Of course we can see the fallacy in their thinking. Had they taken the time—and it wouldn't have taken long— all of their objections could have easily been removed, and they could have believed on Jesus as the Christ to the salvation of their souls. But they preferred to hold to their superficial reasoning. They refused to look more deeply into the matter.

We see their mistake repeated again and again in our generation, as people allow superficial objections to prevent them from seeing such things as the necessity of baptism ("What about the thief on the cross?"), or the error of instrumental music ("David worshiped with instruments"), or the wrong of institutionalism ("The Bible doesn't say 'how'"), or the error of infant baptism ("Weren't whole households baptized?"). Then we wonder if some of our own convictions could possibly be founded upon some shallow reasoning which we have heard and accepted at face value. Is it possible that we have failed to dig more deeply into some Bible subject for fear (unconsciously, maybe) that a more thorough study might lead to unpopular conclusions?

The real reasons behind the Jews' rejection of Jesus: (1) They were not concerned for honoring God, but sought for honor among themselves (John 5.39-47), and (2) they had blinded eyes and hardened hearts (John 12.40). This is frightening! Could such things be true of any of us? The point is this: we can either satisfy ourselves on the basis of superficial thinking or we can seek to honor and please God by opening our eyes and hearts, digging more deeply into His word, and finding a sure foundation on which to build our convictions. It's our choice, but if we are wise, we will dig deep, and lay our foundation on the solid rock of truth.

The Hard Line

Few men are more conservative by nature than is this writer. His inclination is to accept the hard line on just about every question, and he understands the thinking of others who tend to do the same. But one thing we must all learn is that the hard line is not always the right line. The hard line among the early Christians was to oppose the eating of meats (Rom 14.2) and good arguments could be offered for that position. For instance, how could one know that the meat he was eating had not been sacrificed to idols? And how had the animal been killed? Was it possible that the animal had been strangled? Besides, certain meats had been forbidden by the law, and it was still difficult for some Jews to eat those meats with a clear conscience. The "safe" course was just not to eat meats at all. That was the hard line, but the hard line was not the right line.

Oh, if someone wanted to hold to this hard line as his own private standard of conduct, that was all right. He could refrain from eating meats if he considered that to be the safe course for him. And no one was to despise him for following that course of action (Rom 14.3). In fact, if he maintained serious doubts concerning eating meats, he was warned not to eat (Rom 14.23). But he had no right to command others to follow this hard line and abstain from meats. To do so was to "depart from the faith, giving heed to deceiving spirits and doctrines of demons" (1 Tim 4.1-5). The hard line was just not the right line.

Truth on any question cannot be determined by following the hard line, the soft line, or the "middle of the road" line; it can only be determined by a "thus saith the Lord." We must preach whatever the Bible teaches, speaking "as the oracles of God" (1 Pet 4.11). If this leads us to follow what the world or even other Christians consider to be the hard line on any question, so be it. The faithful preacher will "preach the word," knowing that "the time will come when they will not endure sound doctrine, but according to their own desires, because they have itching ears, they will heap up for themselves teachers" (2 Tim 4.2-3).

On the other hand, we know of some "hard lines" which brethren have taken that just cannot be sustained by scripture. We might acknowledge them to be "safe" and consequently **all right** for their own personal standard of conduct. We might grant the right to explain to others why this hard line is being followed. **In fact, this writer has in many instances adopted those same standards for his own standard of conduct.** But let us never be guilty of **commanding** that which God has not taught, thus binding on earth what God has never bound in heaven. The hard line is not always the right line.

Would You Withdraw?

"Would you withdraw from a brother who differs with you on this matter?" This is a question that seems to be arising with increasing frequency whenever brethren disagree.

It is a question that must be considered seriously by sincere Christians, for there are false teachers who must be marked and avoided. "Now I urge you, brethren, note those who cause divisions and offenses, contrary to the doctrine which you learned, and avoid them" (Rom 16.17). "Whoever transgresses and does not abide in the doctrine of Christ does not have God. He who abides in the doctrine of Christ has both the Father and the Son. If anyone comes to you and does not bring this doctrine, do not receive him into your house nor greet him; for he who greets him shares in his evil deeds" (2 John 9-11). There comes the point when we can no longer extend the right hand of fellowship, for we are convinced that there are men among us who are leading the church into apostasy. What we would build up, they would tear down. What we would tear down, they would try to build up. How can we lend our encouragement and endorsement to such men?

Sometimes the question of fellowship is used, however, to try to discredit a man before he is given a fair hearing. A man presents his convictions concerning the celebration of Christmas, or the woman's head covering, or a Christian's participation in carnal warfare, or the right of a woman to raise questions in a mixed Bible class, or concerning any number of other matters that pertain to personal, individual conduct, and the first question raised in reply might be, "Would you withdraw from a brother who differs with you on this matter?" The raising of such a question doesn't answer a single argument, but it surely does put the teacher on the spot. If he answers "yes" to the question, he is marked as a divider of the church over his opinions. If he answers "no," his sincerity in really believing what he has presented is questioned. The poor man is caught either way. He is discredited and embarrassed, **but his position, whether it is true or false, is not answered**!!! Sometimes it is easier to discredit a man and prejudice an audience against him than it is to answer his arguments.

We cannot fellowship those who are leading the church into apostasy. Nor can we fellowship those who are causing divisions and offenses contrary to the doctrine of Christ. But must we break fellowship with one another over every difference that might arise, even those pertaining to personal, individual conduct? We hope not, for such action would split the church into a hundred splinters.

Surely there is room for longsuffering in such matters. And surely we can develop a sense of fairness in our discussions of such differences. Prejudicial questions and unfair tactics have no place in discussions between sincere Christians.

Mixed Swimming

On the question of mixed swimming there are three possible positions:

1. **It is right**. If this position is correct, mixed swimming is right, whether one be an elder, deacon, preacher, or whatever, whether one is in Florida or Alabama, whether one is among friends at home or among strangers in some distant city.

2. **It is wrong**. If this position is correct, mixed swimming is wrong, whoever one might be, and wherever he might be, whether at home or on vacation. It is wrong for the teenager as well as for the adult.

3. **It is right, but the principle of Romans 14 is applicable**. According to this principle, one should forgo the practice if thereby his "brother stumbles or is offended or is made weak" (14.21). If this third position be correct, the question is in reality a matter of indifference, one that involves no inherent wrong, one in which every man is to be "fully convinced in his own mind" (14.5). If this position is correct, opponents of mixed swimming are in reality "weak" brethren, to be received, "but not to disputes over doubtful things" (14.1). Those who are willing to forgo legitimate rights for the sake of their influence among brethren are to be commended, but is this really the correct position? Are those who oppose mixed swimming weak brethren, objecting to that which in reality is wholesome and good?

The issue centers upon the question of dress. Is a swimsuit justifiable in light of 1 Timothy 2.9? "In like manner also, that women adorn themselves in modest apparel, with shamefacedness and sobriety...." The following definitions should be helpful:

Modest: "orderly, well arranged, decent" (W.E. Vine).

Shamefastness: "a sense of shame, modesty" (W.E. Vine).

"Shamefastness is that modesty which is 'fast' or rooted in the character" (Davies, *Bible English*, p. 12). The word "fast" means "firmly fixed." The "bedfast" person is firmly fixed in his bed. The shamefast person is firmly fixed in a sense of shame or modesty. Shamefastness is the opposite of boldness or brazenness.

Sobriety: "denotes soundness of mind" (W.E. Vine). "It is that habitual inner self-government, with its constant rein on all the passions and desires, which would hinder the temptation to these from arising…"(Trench).

Combining these definitions, we conclude that a woman must dress modestly, decently, with a sense of shame or modesty that is rooted, firmly fixed, in her character, not with boldness, in such a way that anyone looking at her would have the impression that here is a woman who keeps a constant rein on all her passions and desires. These definitions force us to accept position two. And while we do not desire to be ugly or rude, we do ask with candor those who accept either of the other two positions, "If a swimsuit would be acceptable in the light of this passage, please tell us what attire would be unacceptable?"

The Indwelling Of the Spirit

Few people would question the fact that the Holy Spirit in some way dwells within the Christian. Paul wrote to the saints in Corinth: "Or do you not know that your body is the temple of the Holy Spirit who is in you…" (1 Cor 6.19). He further wrote, "Now if anyone does not have the Spirit of Christ, he is not His" (Rom 8.9). There is considerable disagreement, however, as to **how** the Spirit dwells within a Christian. It is not our aim in this short article to deal with that issue, but we do want to suggest three facts that must be remembered as one studies the question.

1. The age of miracles is past. The only people in the gospel age who ever performed miracles were those who either received the baptism of the Holy Spirit (Acts 2.1-4; 10.44-46) or received spiritual gifts through the laying on of the apostles' hands (Acts 8.5-23; 19.1-7). No one receives either of these today. The purpose

of the miracles was to reveal and confirm truth (1 Cor 2.7-13; Mark 16.19-20). Since all truth has been revealed (John 16.13), there is no further need for miracles. One's conclusion, therefore, concerning the indwelling of the Spirit must be compatible with this fact.

2. The Christian is led by the Spirit through the scriptures, the word of God (Psa 119.105; 2 Tim 3.16-17; Eph 3.3-4). He does not have some inner voice, separate from the scriptures, that somehow guides him into infallible conclusions in relation to truth and right. Nor is there anything in the scriptures that suggests that God's providence somehow works through the indwelling of the Spirit. Consequently, one makes a serious mistake if he interprets his feelings or subjective thinking as some kind of message provided by the indwelling Spirit.

3. Statements concerning the indwelling of the Spirit were not placed in the scriptures as problems to be wrestled with. They were placed there for one's assurance and consolation. A Christian sustains a very close fellowship with deity—so close that it can be said that he dwells in deity and deity dwells in him. In persecution, trials, temptations, and death his recognition of this close relationship sustains him and helps him to become triumphant in Christ. The apostles never felt the need to explain how this indwelling takes place. Pentecostalism and other misconceptions concerning the Holy Spirit force the Christian of this generation to be concerned with this problem. If, however, statements concerning the indwelling of the Spirit become primarily to him a problem to be wrestled with, if his obsession with the "how" of the Spirit's indwelling blinds him to the "fact" of that indwelling, he makes a serious mistake and may fail to find the joy and consolation that should be gained through the Lord's promise.

Differences will continue to exist, but a constant remembrance of these three facts should protect any one of us from dangerous conclusions in relation to this question.

The Blessing of an Absolute Commitment

There are two relationships in life in which God demands absolute commitment: one's relationship with Christ as a Christian and one's relationship with his companion in marriage. One can give up his citizenship for another, or his job, or his residence, or his congregational affiliation. But one's commitments to Christ and to his companion are lifetime commitments. Desertion of either results in God's disapproval.

When one becomes a Christian, he pledges his allegiance to Christ as his Lord and King. Persecution may come, or discouragement, or temptation, or church troubles, but he promises to be faithful—faithful as long as he lives. Similarly, when one marries, he pledges to his companion his love and faithfulness "so long as they both shall live." Problems may arise, or sickness, or financial difficulties, or pressure from family members, or misunderstandings, but he promises to be faithful. He will not depart. Divorce will be unthinkable. He is committed to his companion—he is hers and she is his—and the commitment is absolute.

God's will concerning the permanence of marriage is clearly revealed. In marriage, a man **leaves** his father and mother and **cleaves** to his wife (Gen 2.24). They are **bound** (Rom 7.2-3). They are **joined together** by God and are not to be **put asunder** (Matt 19.6). They become **one flesh** (Matt 19.6). One cannot think of stronger terms to describe permanence of relationship. No wonder Malachi would say that God hates divorce (Mal 2.16).

The greatest happiness man can experience upon this earth is found in these two realms of absolute commitment. Happiness is not found in half-commitment. A man who is constantly considering other jobs, never becoming committed to his present job, is an unsettled man, torn between options. So it is with that person who tries to serve the Lord with semi-commitment. He is bored and disinterested, having just enough religion to make him miserable. He tries to hold to the world with one hand and to the Lord with the other and finds joy in neither. One needs but to look at the apostles and earliest disciples, on the other hand, to see that absolute commitment, the kind of commitment that can accept persecution and render sacrifice, is a basic element of joy in the Lord (Acts 2.41-47; 5.40-42; 16.25).

So it is with marriage. God knew that happiness in marriage could be found only in absolute commitment. So he decreed through the apostle Paul, "Let each man have his own wife, and let each woman have her own husband"—one man for one woman until death separates them (1 Cor 7.2). His decree may be troublesome to those who have, in the past, ignored His teaching (the consequences of sin are always terrible—Gal 6.7-8), but it is for the good of mankind, proceeding from God who commands for our good (Deut 10.13).

1. **Absolute commitment provides trust in marriage.** The husband does not have to worry about his wife's faithfulness to him, nor does the wife have to worry about the husband, for their commitment to one another is open and obvious. Because of the openness of their commitment, temptation to be unfaithful is practically non-existent. The half-committed, on the other hand, will be frequently tempted, for temptation is inherent in partial commitment.

2. **Absolute commitment provides security in marriage.** Security is an outgrowth of trust and permanency. It is when one doubts the strength and permanency of his relationship with another that he feels insecure.

3. **Absolute commitment provides a settled life in marriage.** Gone are the troubled, unsettled, insecure days of courtship, replaced by a lasting, secure relationship with one's partner. Naomi described this settled life beautifully when she said of Ruth, "**My daughter, shall I not seek security for you, that it may be well with you?**" (Ruth 3.1)

4. **Absolute commitment provides a solid foundation upon which to build in marriage.** Without this foundation, no quality home can ever be built.

Gus Nichols once wrote that he and his wife had been present for Bible classes the previous Sunday and for both worship periods. He went on to say that they had not made their decision on that Sunday, but had made that decision forty years before when they had first become Christians, and that, in being present for all services, they were just being true to the commitment they had made forty years before. Similarly, I pillowed my head beside my wife last night and awoke this morning by her side. If the Lord wills, I shall do so again tonight and shall continue to do so as long as we both shall live. Not that we are just now making that decision, for we made that decision twenty-five years ago and are merely being true to that lifelong commitment we made so many years in the past.

"Marriage is honorable among all, and the bed undefiled; but fornicators and adulterers God will judge" (Heb 13.4).

Building Happy Homes

Is it true that Christians of the present generation are far more hesitant to marry than those of past generations? We occasionally hear such an observation expressed, and we tend to agree with it. We are acquainted with many "very eligible" young people in their late 20s and early 30s who don't seem to be even close to marrying.

The reasons for this development may be many, but we can't help but wonder if some are not just afraid of marriage. They have heard so many sermons on divorce and its causes. They have observed so many marriages fall apart, even among leaders of the church in whom they had placed great confidence. They have seen couples live in total misery while staying together. It is no wonder that they have become disillusioned and doubts that there is such a thing as a happy home. One observant young man once said to this writer, "Why doesn't someone preach a sermon on 'Happiness in Marriage'?" Many may be in need of reassurance.

Now, we are not campaigning for everyone to marry—that's a very personal matter—and especially we would not encourage anyone to rush into marriage. But Christians should not have a fatalistic view of marriage. God ordained marriage for our good and happiness. "He who finds a wife finds a good thing, and obtains favor from the LORD" (Prov 18.22). God said in the beginning, "Therefore a man shall leave his father and mother and be joined to his wife, and they shall become one flesh" (Gen 2.24).

The blessedness of marriage can be seen in that it is a giving relationship. One gives materially, emotionally, sexually—in short, one gives himself. In marriage "I" becomes "we"; "my" becomes "our." The two are joined by God, and become one.

Two **Christians** with God's help can build a beautiful relationship, a relationship which neither sickness, hard times, nor forced separations can sever. The foundation for that relationship is laid in complete submission to God's teaching combined with a mutual love and respect for one another. Each experience subsequently shared— whether of joy or of sorrow—becomes new material that adds to the total structure, so that with each passing year the relationship finds itself more tightly bound than ever before. This is marriage as God would have it. Within such a marriage Christians can find joy, happiness, security, and vital help for eternity. They live together, they share together, they pray together, they laugh together, they weep together, they grow old together, and finally they are "heirs together of the grace of life" (I Pet 3.7).

So, my young friends, be cautious, but don't be afraid. Don't expect the impossible, but do expect the joy of loving and being loved. Don't expect a problem-free marriage, but do expect to work out your problems through mutual respect for God and His word. There is happiness in marriage for two who are truly God's children.

Six Steps to a Broken Home

A home is seldom destroyed "overnight." Its destruction is usually the result of certain fatal steps taken over a lengthy period of time. In these days, when so many homes are crumbling, we would do well to examine our own marital relationships, to see if we have begun to travel the road to inevitable breakup. The following steps lead down that road.

1. **Selfishness**. This may be the number one enemy of a happy home life. Each person is doing his own thing. Neither is willing to give up what he wants to do that wholesome activities may be en-

joyed together. Each is seeking his own satisfaction in materialism, in sexual activities, or in time spent with relatives with little concern for the partner's satisfaction in these matters. The long road is begun.

2. **Intolerance.** Faults in one's partner begin to show up that somehow had been hidden during the courtship period. Or, if the faults were evident; they become far more irritating in a day-to-day, living together, relationship. Gradually those faults are magnified. Nagging begins. Each decides that he has made a terrible mistake in his marriage.

3. **Resignation.** Both parties become resigned to their situation. "We've made our bed; we will just have to lie in it," they think. No further effort is made to build a happy home. Communication virtually ceases. Love begins to fade, and in many cases gives way to bitterness.

4. **End of sexual relations.** The communication barrier soon affects the sexual relationship, and the couple find themselves no longer enjoying and fulfilling this God-given purpose in marriage. They have allowed their marriage to deteriorate into a mere housekeeping relationship. Such people may be easy pushovers for the next step.

5. **Adultery.** Temptation can arise so unexpectedly, and many a person whose physical needs are not being met at home may yield to the temptation. Rationalization comes easy in such cases: The person feels he has never gotten a "fair shake" at home; he deserves this newfound attention; this is true love (?); he is sure someone understands him for the first time. How deceptive sin is! Considerable time has passed since our couple took those first steps toward a broken home, but now their journey is completed. Only one other step remains.

6. **Separation.** The thing that has obviously destroyed this home is sin, but not just the sin of adultery. Selfishness, intolerance, lack of love, bitterness, and failure to satisfy physical needs (whenever possible) all constitute sin. We can come to but one conclusion. Sin is the cause of broken homes. It may be sin on the part of one or both parties, but a home is broken because of sin.

A Richly Blessed Family

"Pity the Smith family. Poor things, they have to keep the preacher every time the church plans a meeting. And Christians are always stopping in at their place. And they are about the only people in the church that ever invite people in after services. I just wouldn't put up with it myself...."

Spare your pity! The Smiths are a richly blessed family. Oh, occasionally they entertain some ungrateful scoundrel, but the blessings of hospitality far outweigh the problems.

The Bible speaks of some wonderfully blessed people along these lines. For instance, we do not pity Mary and Martha for "having" to have Jesus in their home; we pity those who, not wanting Jesus, were deprived of this blessing. We do not pity Mary the mother of John Mark, in whose home "many were gathered together praying"; we pity those homes where Christians never assemble for Bible study and prayer. We do not pity Philemon who was to prepare lodging for Paul; we would love to have Paul as a guest in our home. Christians need to learn the joy and blessings which come to those who are hospitable.

"We are hospitable," someone says, "we often have friends from church in our home for get-togethers and parties." That's fine! We encourage this! But Bible hospitality goes beyond having **friends** in for an evening which is at least partially for our own **selfish** enjoyment. "I was a stranger and you took Me in," Jesus will say in the judgment (Matt 25.35). Gaius was commended for helping "brethren" and "strangers" who were traveling for the Lord's name's sake, and was told by John, "If you send them forward on their journey in a manner worthy of God, you will do well" (3 John 5-7). Further, the Bible teaches that we become partakers in **evil** deeds of **false** teachers when we receive them into our houses (2 John 9-11). But does this not imply that we become partakers in the **good** deeds of **faithful** teachers when we show them hospitality?

A Christian will want to make friends with other Christians and consequently will plan enjoyable evenings with close friends in his home. But the hospitable Christian will also use his home for conducting Bible classes, entertaining visiting preachers and other workers for the Lord, getting acquainted with newcomers in the church, comforting the bereaved and troubled, and for every good work.

Our homes are blessings from the Lord. We must not use them selfishly, but rather to His glory. The result will be an occasional scratch on a chair, or a stain on the carpet, or a chipped glass—really a small price to pay, though, for the warmth that comes to the home from new friends, good influences, rich Bible discussions, participation in the Lord's work, and the satisfaction of knowing that one is pleasing God and preparing himself for eternity. No, it's not the Smiths whom we pity; it's those who do not know the joy of hospitality.

Choosing a Companion

A happy home begins with a wise choice of a marriage partner. We therefore submit the following questions as a guide for our young people as they seek out their companion for life.

1. **Is this person eligible for marriage?** There are those who have a right to marry according to the laws of our state, but who do not have a right to marry according to the law of God. God's authority is supreme, and the Christian must abide by His law whenever there is a conflict between His law and governmental law.

God's law is that only those who are divorced for the cause of fornication have a right to remarry. "And I say to you, whoever divorces his wife, except for sexual immorality, and marries another, commits adultery; and whoever marries her who is divorced commits adultery" (Matt 19.9). If one's marriage partner is guilty of marital infidelity, he can put that partner away **for that cause**, and marry another. If the divorce is for any other cause, he is ineligible for marriage.

2. **Is this person a Christian?** Many problems can arise when a Christian is married to a non-Christian, especially when it is the wife who is the Christian. Before any young lady marries a non-Christian, she should consider the following problems which often face the Christian in a mixed marriage.

a. **Problems in attending services.** She should ask herself, "What will I do if my husband some Lord's Day drives away in the car, leaving me with no transportation to the services?" "What will I do if my husband announces that his company is moving us to some city where no church of the Lord meets?" Many women have faced these problems.

b. **Problems in giving.** The young lady loves the Lord and His work, and wants to give liberally in support of it. Her husband, however, does not share her convictions. He feels that a dollar is plenty to give.

c. **Problems in training children.** Some have succeeded in bringing up their children to be Christians without the help of their companions. Eunice succeeded with Timothy. But the influence of a father is great, and many are the women who have not been able to overcome this influence to see their children become Christians.

d. **Problems in overcoming the influence of one's companion.** Marrying with the hope of reforming one's companion is a dangerous thing. Often the companion is lifted to a higher standard, but seldom to the standard of a Christian. Instead, as the non-Christian's standards are raised, the Christian's standards are lowered, so that the two meet somewhere in between. The young lady should realize that the man she marries will be the greatest influence of an earthly nature on her life, and she should ask herself, "Will this man help me to go to heaven?"

e. **Emotional problems.** Recently a godly woman, having just received word of her husband's death in an automobile accident, cried, "Why couldn't it have been me or one of the children, for my husband was not ready to die?"

Is the reader thinking she will convert her husband after marriage? She may be able to do so, but statistics show that her chances are not very good. The risk is too great. The only safe course is for Christians to marry Christians.

3. **Does this person possess strength of character?** Many boys and girls seem to want to do right but are just too easily influenced by their associates or by the circumstances which surround them. Such weakness of character does not make for a good marriage

partner. If one wants a happy home, he should choose a companion who is dependable, whose word can be trusted, and who has the strength to do right, even when all around him are doing wrong.

After all, if that young man or woman lies to his parents or employer, he will someday lie to you. If he is excessively jealous and possessive during courtship, he will manifest the same weaknesses after marriage. If he is quick-tempered—or flirty—or a "showoff"—or a spendthrift—or a "tightwad"—now, he will be after marriage. One cannot marry a moral weakling and expect a happy home.

Yes, there will be faults and eccentricities that must be accepted and tolerated in any happy relationship between two people. But there are certain conditions that are practically intolerable, and we hope that this article will help some young person avoid such.

Qualities That Make For a Good Wife

What qualities should a young man look for in the girl that he would marry? What qualities should the girl look for in the young man? What qualities should we who are already married be demonstrating in our own lives? The book of Ruth provides some answers to these questions as it tells of the marriage of two wonderful people, Ruth and Boaz. The following qualities can be seen in Ruth, making her an ideal wife for Boaz.

1. **She was loyal.** The words, "Wherever you go, I will go; and wherever you lodge, I will lodge; your people shall be my people, and your God, my God…" were not originally the sentiment expressed by a bride to her husband, but were words of a loyal daughter-in-law (Ruth) to her mother-in-law (Naomi). But the loyalty expressed by Ruth in those beautiful words to her mother-in-law was the kind of loyalty that would later make her a wonderful wife to Boaz.

2. **She was hard-working.** Having arrived in a strange land with her mother-in-law, Ruth recognized that some provision had to be made for their physical sustenance. So she went out gleaning for corn; i.e., she picked up whatever grain was dropped along the way by the reapers. It just "happened" that the field in which she gleaned was that of Boaz.

3. **She was unselfish.** She not only gleaned for herself; she was also providing for her mother-in-law.

4. **She was God-fearing.** Ruth had been brought up in the land of Moab and had been taught to serve the gods of the Moabites. Through her first husband and in-laws, however, she had learned of the one true God and had come to serve Him. The death of her husband had not affected her loyalty to God, for true loyalty to God transcends death, life, parents, or whatever. This fear of God on the part of Ruth was particularly attractive to Boaz, who, on his first meeting with her, commended her: "The LORD repay your work, and a full reward be given you by the LORD God of Israel, under whose wings you have come for refuge" (Ruth 2.12).

5. **She was grateful.** This beautiful quality, so rare in our own society, shone unmistakably in the life of Ruth, as she, in response to the kindness of Boaz, "fell on her face, bowed down to the ground, and said to him, Why have I found favor in your eyes, that you should take notice of me, since I am a foreigner " (Ruth 2.10).

6. **She was more concerned for quality than for physical attractiveness in a husband.** Indications are that Boaz was considerably older than Ruth. But Boaz was a near kinsman to Ruth's first husband, which, along with his moral and spiritual qualities, made him far more suitable than one who might be closer to her own age. Ruth's recognition of this and her desire to have Boaz as her husband again evoked a response of praise from the lips of Boaz: "Blessed are you of the LORD, my daughter! For you have shown more kindness at the end than at the beginning, in that you did not go after young men, whether poor or rich "(Ruth 3.10).

7. **She was morally pure**. It could be said of Ruth in a general way: "For all the city of my people know that you are a virtuous woman" (Ruth 4.11). But circumstances, recorded in the book of Ruth itself, provided a specific occasion for her and Boaz to demonstrate just how morally pure they really were. The occasion we speak of resulted when Ruth, mistakenly believing that Boaz was the nearest relative to her husband, and consequently believing that she had every right to become his wife (read Deut 25.5-10), went in the dark of night to Boaz with full intentions of becoming his wife

that night. There was just one problem: he was not the nearest relative and they therefore had no right to become husband and wife until legal requirements could be met. Although they were alone at night, possessed with a mutual love, and having full intentions of becoming husband and wife as soon as possible, they maintained their moral purity, leaving a good example for all who would follow afterward. "Marriage is honorable among all, and the bed undefiled; but fornicators and adulterers God will judge" (Heb 13.4).

We are quite sure that if there were more "Ruths" in this world there would be far fewer divorces. What about it, girls? Are you seeking to be a "Ruth"? And, boys, would a "Ruth" be attractive to you? Nothing is said of Ruth's physical appearance, but she was a beautiful woman, for she had a beautiful character.

The Bible teaches that such a woman is of great value, for: "Who can find a virtuous wife? For her worth is far above rubies" (Prov 31.10). The young man who finds such a wife "finds a good thing, and obtains favor from the LORD" (Prov 18.22).

Qualities That Make For a Good Husband

As Ruth provides a good example of the qualities that make for a good wife (see accompanying article), Boaz demonstrates the qualities that a girl ought to seek in the young man who is to be her husband.

1. **He was God-fearing**. Especially impressive is the fact that his fear of God influenced every relationship in life. He greeted those who worked for him with the words, "The LORD be with you," and they replied, "The LORD bless you" (Ruth 2.4). His fear of God obviously influenced his relationship with Ruth. Such spiritual qualities are essential if one is to be a good husband and father.

2. **He was a good provider**. He owned land, and personally accepted the responsibility of overseeing the reaping and threshing of his crops.

3. **He was kind to the needy**. Not only did he allow Ruth to glean in his fields (the law demanded that he do this—(Deut 24.19), but he encouraged her to do so, and provided food, water, and protec-

tion from harm for her throughout the time she worked there. And he even went beyond this to tell his laborers to purposely let some of the grain fall so Ruth could gather that which would be sufficient for her and her mother-in-law (Ruth 2.15-16).

4. **He recognized quality in one who was poor.** When we view Ruth, we see only those beautiful qualities that characterized her life. But Boaz could see more than that. He could see her poor clothing and lowly circumstances; he could see the menial work she was doing. Boaz could have easily been blinded to Ruth's inner beauty by the obvious poverty with which she was surrounded. But Boaz was a perceptive man who could judge character, not on the basis of material wealth, but on the basis of inner purity and godliness.

Because of this, he found and recognized a real jewel who later became his wife.

5. **He was law-abiding.** Knowing he was not the nearest relative to Ruth's former husband, and knowing that consequently he had no legal or God-given right to her, he refused to take her for his wife until legal and divinely-ordained requirements could be met.

People of our age need to learn that there are those who are ineligible for marriage, and that legal eligibility does not necessarily establish eligibility in God's sight. Only three classes of people have a right to marry: (a) those who have never married, (b) those whose companions are dead, and (c) those who have put away their companions for the cause of fornication (Matt 19.9). Marriage on the part of any other results in the formation of an adulterous union that does not have divine approval.

6. **He was morally pure.** He actually took the lead in seeing to it that he and Ruth maintained moral purity (see previous article).

There is nothing wrong with a young man's being handsome or physically strong. But such qualities have little bearing on the kind of husband he will be. Spiritual strength, a willingness to work, kindness, respect for authority, strength of character, truthfulness, self-respect, etc., are the virtues that make for a good husband. Boaz had these virtues. There are young men today who have them, and they are the young men that should be attractive to Christian girls.

Marriage can result in great happiness or great misery. For those who carefully choose their mates and work toward building their homes on the sure foundation of God's word, marriage brings happiness. But for those who look on marriage lightly and choose their mates solely on the basis of physical attraction, marriage frequently results in misery and disillusionment. We wish all our young readers the very best, and trust that with God's help they can find true happiness, both in this life and in the life to come.

Understanding Husbands

"You husbands likewise, live with your wives in an understanding way…" (1 Pet 3.7, NASB).

A good husband is concerned for his wife's welfare and is understanding in relation to all her needs.

1. **Her material needs.** He understands that his wife would like a new outfit occasionally just as he does, that she would enjoy some spending money that she can "call her own," and that she would enjoy an occasional break from the kitchen. Understanding these things, he places her material needs and those of his children ahead of his own.

2. **Her health needs.** He does not complain when his wife needs to see a doctor or when her failing health requires extensive medical treatment. He provides the best care for her that he can afford and he does so cheerfully.

3. **Her social needs.** A good woman is hospitable. She recognizes the need for good companionships for all her family. She wants her home to be a place where fellow Christians feel comfortable and welcome. An understanding husband recognizes these needs too and often gives up his own personal interests for the sake of his family's social needs. Also, he plans trips to visit with his wife's parents and others in her family. In fact, her people become his people.

4. **Her spiritual needs.** A good man provides spiritual leadership for his family. He not only attends worship periods and Bible classes with his family, he makes the home a spiritual center itself. He prays with his family. He reads and discusses the scriptures with

them. At various times—while riding in the car, or walking through the woods, or sitting around the dinner table—he exhorts and encourages his wife and children to be godly in behavior and spiritual in their outlook. He is concerned for his own example before his family and does not hesitate to say "I'm sorry" when he is aware of wrongdoing on his part.

5. **Her physical needs**. A husband and wife are to render "the affection due" to each other (1 Cor 7.2-5), satisfying one another's sexual needs. Neither should be overly demanding of the other; neither should "deprive" the other. The man who becomes "married" to his job and neglectful to his wife makes a serious mistake.

6. **Her emotional needs**. An understanding husband appreciates his wife and expresses by both word and deed his appreciation and love. It is said of the "virtuous woman" of Proverbs 31: "Her children rise up and call her blessed; her husband also, and he praises her. Many daughters have done well, but you excel them all" (28-29).

God has given to man the position of headship in the home and the responsibility of showing himself worthy of that position. Many are failing—miserably failing! How applicable the exhortation of David becomes: "Prove yourself a man!"

What God Hath Joined Together

Only three classes of people are eligible for marriage according to Bible teaching: (1) Those who have never married, (2) Those whose partners are dead, and (3) Those who have put away their partners because of fornication (marital infidelity).

Jesus' teaching concerning divorce and remarriage is clear: "And I say to you, whoever divorces his wife, except for sexual immorality, and marries another, commits adultery; and whoever marries her who is divorced commits adultery" (Matt 19.9).

When two eligible people are married, the Bible describes them as being "bound" (Rom 7.2), "one flesh" (Matt 19.6), "cleaving to one another" (Matt 19.5), and such are not to be put asunder, for: "Therefore what God has joined together, let not man separate" (Matt 19.6).

When one divorces his companion for any cause other than fornication and marries another, he enters into an adulterous union with that one whom he marries.

"It is not lawful for [him] to have her" (Matt 14.4). Neither the passing of time, the strengthening of affection, or the birth of children can make it lawful. They are in adultery in the sight of God.

Forgiveness for this sinful relationship can be received in the same manner as for any other sin, through repentance and obedience to the gospel. But there's the rub! Repentance demands a cessation of the sin being repented of. If one repents of lying, he must cease his lying. If one repents of stealing, he must cease his stealing. In the same manner, when one repents of his adultery, he must cease his adultery. Thus, when one who has been living in an adulterous union obeys the gospel, he must terminate that adulterous relationship. This teaching seems hard in today's society, but it is Bible teaching on this subject.

Obviously, the best course of action is to avoid this emotionally charged predicament. "An ounce of prevention is worth a pound of cure." Those who are eligible for marriage should date others who are eligible, avoiding close companionships with those who are ineligible. "But we are just friends," someone may be thinking as he goes out with one who is ineligible for marriage, "I wouldn't think of marrying this person." Such thinking is extremely dangerous. We know of a number of people whose lives are now ruined because they saw no danger in being "friends" with those whom they could not marry with God's approval. The only safe course is for those who are eligible for marriage to keep company with others who are eligible for marriage. To do otherwise is to play with fire.

Those who are married must recognize the permanency of their relationship, and work diligently to make their homes happy and successful. Removing from their minds the possibility of divorce, they must work out their problems with love, patience, and the help of God.

But we do urge those who are presently in adulterous relationships to have the faith and courage to sever their adulterous ties and to serve the Lord. The Lord will bless those who do so, and "Heaven will surely be worth it all."

God Hates Divorce

"I'm getting a divorce, but I don't plan to marry again." These words are being heard with increasing frequency. Usually the spokesman is thinking that God allows the right to divorce, but would disapprove remarriage. The truth is, however: **Divorce itself is sinful unless it is for the cause of fornication**.

Consider Matthew 19.3-6. The question originally asked Jesus by the Pharisees was not concerning remarriage, but concerning divorce: "Is it lawful for a man to divorce his wife for just any reason?" Jesus' reply to that question: "Therefore what God has joined together, let not man separate." It was only after further questioning that Jesus discussed the problem of remarriage and adultery.

Consider Malachi 2:16. "For the LORD God of Israel says that He hates divorce." Even under the old covenant God did not approve of indiscriminate divorce. It is likely that the "tears" of verse 13 which covered "the altar" and caused the Lord to refuse their offering were the tears of those who had been wrongfully put away.

Consider Matthew 5:32. "Whoever divorces his wife for any reason except sexual immorality causes her to commit adultery." Observe the words "causes her" or "maketh her" (ASV). This writer understands this verse to say that if one divorces his wife for any cause other than fornication, **he places her** in a position of temptation to commit adultery and shares the guilt when she does commit adultery. On the other hand, if he puts her away for the cause of fornication, he has put her away legitimately and shares no guilt in whatever adultery she may subsequently commit.

Consider 1 Corinthians 7.10. "Now to the married I command, yet not I but the Lord: A wife is not to depart from her husband." Observe the word "command," or "charge" (ASV). The following verse (v 11) does not negate or nullify this command, but simply recognizes that one might disobey the Lord's command (in which case he sins—1 John 3.4), and states his options if he has disobeyed.

Not only does the Lord command husband and wife to live together, but He commands them to meet one another's physical needs (1 Cor 7.3-5) and to love one another (Eph 5.25; Tit 2.4-5). If one companion in a marriage fails along these lines, the other must still be obedient to God, seeking to be what God would have him (or her) to be in the marriage relationship. Never should the thought of divorce or separation ever enter the mind unless fornication occurs.

We are not suggesting that divorce itself is "adultery," but we are saying that divorce for any cause other than fornication is sin. Christians must not be influenced by the loose standards that prevail in the world in which they live.

Challenging Adulterers

Tom is a great personal worker, but he's run into a snag. The couple he's been studying with seemed to be on the verge of responding when Tom learned that they were involved in an adulterous marriage. Poor Tom! He's so disappointed. "There is no use working with this couple anymore," he thinks, "you know they wouldn't separate and break their adulterous relationship."

They wouldn't what??? People who want to serve the Lord and go to heaven are willing to give up **anything** to do so. The early Christians never hesitated to challenge lost people to give up **whatever** stood between them and heaven. The Corinthian converts had given up their fornication, idolatry, drunkenness, homosexual practices, and other sinful activities (1 Cor 6.9-11). Of course they had. They wanted to go to heaven. Paul did not hesitate to tell those who were married to unbelievers, "But if the unbeliever departs, **let him depart**" (1 Cor 7.15). Paul apparently thought there were people who would be willing to live celibate lives for the rest of their days if that's what it took to go to heaven, and he was not hesitant to challenge them to do so.

But will people really give up **anything** in order to go to heaven? Would Abraham really have given up his only son? Of course he would have! Would Daniel have given up his high position in

Nebuchadnezzar's government? Or Moses the luxury of Pharaoh's palace? Or Saul of Tarsus his potential greatness in the Jews' religion? Or the apostles their lives? Yes, they would, for they wanted to go to heaven.

What enabled these great Bible characters to sacrifice so much for the Lord's cause? Faith! "By faith Abraham..." "By faith Moses..." "I know whom I have believed and am persuaded...." These men through faith could look beyond the cares and suffering of this world to see a "better [country], that is, a heavenly." They believed that heavenly considerations should transcend **all** earthly considerations, and believing, they placed their hands to the plow and never looked back.

What should Tom do in the case of the adulterous couple? One thing for sure, he shouldn't throw up his hands in despair. Rather, he should bring them to love the Lord and want to go to heaven, and if he succeeds, they will break their adulterous relationship. **Wouldn't you?** Wouldn't you be willing to give up your family—if necessary—or anything else, in order to go to heaven? Or is it possible that our judgment of what others would be willing to sacrifice is tainted by our own lack of commitment and sacrifice? Is it possible that we do not have sufficient faith and commitment ourselves to lead others to the salvation of their souls?

"If anyone comes to Me and does not hate his father and mother, wife and children, brothers and sisters, yes, and his own life also, he cannot be My disciple" (Luke 14.26).

The Christian Father

Little difficulty is experienced in thinking of outstanding Bible women in the home: Hannah, Mary, Elizabeth, Jochebed, Eunice. Efforts to think of a comparable list of men, however, are not easy, for many great men of the Bible were failures in their homes: David, Lot, Eli, Samuel, Jacob, etc. A look at the causes of their failure might help our male readers to avoid their mistakes.

1. **Immorality**. David's adultery with Bathsheba and subsequent murder of her husband, Uriah, resulted in the ruin of David's home.

Noah's drunkenness contributed to trouble within his family, thus marring the success with which he had brought up his sons in a society of unparalleled wickedness. Men today, if they live in drunkenness, adultery, and other forms of immorality, cannot hope to be successes in their homes.

2. **Lack of discipline**. Destruction came upon Eli and his family because "his sons made themselves vile, and he did not restrain them" (1 Sam 3.13). The Bible says: "Chasten your son while there is hope, and do not set your heart on his destruction" (Prov 19.18).

3. **Greed**. "Lot lifted his eyes and saw all the plain of Jordan, that it was well watered everywhere...like the garden of the LORD" (Gen 13.10), and, apparently motivated by a desire for material abundance, moved his family into Sodom. The consequences of this sad mistake are well known to our readers. Many Christians today are making the same mistake as they sacrifice their children on the altar of greed, being willing to move their children anywhere for the sake of a promotion or more money.

4. **Partiality**. This oft-committed mistake brought trouble to the home of Isaac, who was partial to Esau while Rebekah was partial to Jacob, and to that of Jacob, who was partial to Joseph. Not only did the family suffer generally in each of these cases, but the favored one suffered especially. Pity the favorite child in any family. He suffers more than anyone else in the family.

What can men do to avoid failure in the home? They can recognize their position of headship in the home. "For the husband is head of the wife, as also Christ is head of the church" (Eph 5.23). Recognizing this, they can develop greater worthiness of this place of headship through increased strength of character and conviction. It is sad to see a godly woman trying to be in subjection to a weak, indecisive, vacillating husband. Men will do well to heed David's counsel to Solomon, "Prove yourself a man" (1 Kgs 2.2).

They can become more thoughtful of their wives and children. Men would do well to turn their attention away from the TV, sportscasts, and newspapers, and spend time with their families.

They can lead the family in prayer, Bible reading, and devotion. They will do well to consider the instructions given to the children of Israel: "And these words which I command you today shall be in your heart. You shall teach them diligently to your children, and shall talk of them when you sit in your house, when you walk by the way, when you lie down, and when you rise up" (Deut 6.6-7).

Many children have never heard their fathers pray; have never even heard them give thanks for the food. Pity those children.

Fathers can pray without ceasing for the Lord's help. The task of bringing up children in the nurture and admonition of the Lord is one of the greatest responsibilities men must face in life. That responsibility should be carried out prayerfully.

Finally, they can develop humility. The following poem, "Two Prayers," written by an unknown author, suggests the humility every father needs.

> Last night my little boy
> Confessed to me
> Some childish wrong;
> And kneeling at my knee
> He prayed with tears;
> "Dear God, make me a man
> Like Daddy—wise and strong;
> I know you can."
> Then while he slept
> I knelt beside his bed,
> Confessed my sins,
> And prayed with bowed head;
> "O God, make me a child,
> Like my child here—
> Pure, guileless,
> Trusting thee with faith sincere."

The Christian Mother

Baxter Walker once wrote the following ad:

"There is an opening for a well-rounded, personable, patient, clean and neat, well-dressed, healthy (this requirement sometimes waived) and attractive individual."

"Long hours, low pay, fair working conditions, few fringe benefits, occasional vacation, no guaranteed holidays. Applicant must have management ability, dietary knowledge, ability to drive, knowledge of etiquette, knowledge of new math is helpful but not required, ability to sew, mechanical knowledge, and must show commitment to the position. No written test required."

The position described is that of motherhood, that difficult role which God has given to the woman.

The Bible description of the virtuous woman of Proverbs 31.10-31 certainly indicates that motherhood is not an easy role. Observe the following from this passage:

1. **Her character**. She is a "virtuous woman." "The heart of her husband safely trusts her."

2. **Her value**. "Her worth is far above rubies."

3. **Her willingness to work**. "She seeks wool and flax, and willingly works with her hands." "She also rises while it is yet night, and provides food for her household and a portion for her maidservants."

4. **Her economy**. "She considers a field and buys it; from her profits she plants a vineyard." Because she manages well, her husband "will have no lack of gain."

5. **Her benevolence**. "She extends her hand to the poor, yes, she reaches out her hands to the needy."

6. **Her unselfishness**. "She is not afraid of snow for her household, for all her household is clothed with scarlet."

7. **Her encouragement to her husband**. "Her husband is known in the gates, when he sits among the elders of the land."

8. **Her wisdom**. "She opens her mouth with wisdom."

9. **Her kind disposition**. "On her tongue is the law of kindness."

10. **Her ability to discipline**. "She watches over the ways of her household."

The mother's role is indeed a difficult one, but the blessings far outweigh the difficulties. Concerning this virtuous woman of Proverbs 31 the scriptures say: "Her children rise up and call her blessed; her husband also, and he praises her. Many daughters have done well, but you excel them all'" (Prov 31.28-29).

And, further, "Charm is deceitful and beauty is passing, but a woman who fears the Lord, she shall be praised" (31.30). This writer knows of no greater need in this world than for women to return to their God-ordained roles. Encouraged by the "equal rights" and "women's lib" movements, and motivated by the desire to "keep up with the Joneses," women have left their homes and children to enter the world of business and secular work. Many dangers face the woman who follows this course. A feeling of independence can develop causing the woman, who now has her own income, to feel superior to her husband and no longer subject to him or dependent on him.

Children can be neglected. They come home from school to an empty house while their friends have "Mother" to welcome them and listen to their stories of the events of the day. When the working mother does come in, she may be so exhausted and frustrated that she can give little time, attention, and love to the children. Her life can gradually become centered upon her job rather than upon her home.

Further, the woman can be influenced by the worldly people with whom she is associated on the job. Many women who never smoked, cursed, or dressed immodestly before they accepted jobs have been influenced to do so after they began working.

It is not our purpose to bring these charges against every woman who ever worked. Indeed, we have known women who, because of unfortunate circumstances, had to work, and, having recognized the potential dangers, have sought to avoid them. We have nothing but admiration for such women. But we believe that all honest people must acknowledge that many problems do exist because so many mothers work, and that **ideally**, the woman's place is in the home, not in public work. Christian women are to be "keepers at home" (Tit 2.4-5, KJV).

Some Things I Want To Teach My Children

"And you, fathers, do not provoke your children to wrath, but bring them up in the training and admonition of the Lord" (Eph 6.4).

In keeping with the instructions of this passage, there are certain things that I want to teach my children.

1. **I want to teach my children proper reverence and respect in the worship periods of the church.** When we meet for worship, we are present before God to worship God. Cornelius understood this as he said, "Now therefore, we are all present before God, to hear all the things commanded you by God" (Acts 10.33). Many people surely have given little thought to this matter. Women talk to each other in the nursery. Young people laugh and talk in the assembly. Children march in an unnecessary parade to the restrooms. Healthy men and women who can be so eager and enthusiastic at an antique auction or a ball game or a school program drag in at the worship periods, flop down listlessly into the pew, and sleep throughout the sermon. Surely these people fail to realize that we are present **before God to worship God.** I hope to teach my children that they are to reverence God, that they are to sit quietly throughout the worship period, that they are to bow their heads in prayer, that they are to participate in the singing, and that they are to avoid creating any unnecessary disturbance during worship.

2. **I want to teach my children to seek first the kingdom of God.** Jesus said, "But seek first the kingdom of God and His righteousness, and all these things (material things of life-BH) shall be added to you" (Matt 6.33). I want my children to know that their growing up to be faithful Christians means more to me than anything else relative to them. Should they excel in sports, make top grades in school, earn Ph.D. degrees, win beauty contests, and live in luxury all their days, but fail to be faithful Christians, and consequently go to hell when they die, I will have failed as a parent.

If my boy wants to play Little League baseball, we must have a talk with his coach **before** we commit ourselves, and explain to the coach that if a conflict arises between my boy's spiritual activities and his baseball activities, his spiritual activities must come first.

Then we must abide by that understanding consistently, whatever pressures may arise to do otherwise. The same principle must apply in school activities, social activities, boy scouts, girl scouts, etc. Further, I hope to bring my children as they grow into maturity to make these decisions on their own. Too many young people hide behind their parents with the convenient "Mother won't let me," instead of standing for their convictions and fighting unashamedly for the Lord. My goal is not to **make** them seek first the kingdom, but to bring them to **want** to seek first the kingdom that they might be pleasing to God.

3. **I want to teach my children respect for authority**: for parental authority (Eph 6.1), for governmental authority (Matt 22.21), **and above all else**, for divine authority (Acts 5.29). A child is to be pitied who is not taught respect for authority when he is very small. He becomes a problem in the Bible class, in school, in the community. Later in life he is a problem on the job; he gets into trouble with the law; and finally he is lost eternally, not having respected God's authority.

There are many things other than these which I hope to teach my children. Space does not permit a discussion of strength of character, honesty, fairness, good manners, etc., all of which I hope to teach my children.

Let no one think of this article as a **boast** of what I shall do; it is the setting forth of **goals**. No one is more conscious of the possibility of failure than am I. But my wife and I pray regularly that God will help us to bring up our children well, and that He will overrule our mistakes. Meanwhile, we try to set a good example before them; we teach them by word of mouth, seeking to abide by those instructions which God gave to Israel: "And these words which I command you today shall be in your heart. You shall teach them diligently to your children, and you shall talk of them when you sit in your house, when you walk by the way, when you lie down, and when you rise up" (Deut 6.6-7); and we try to do this consistently. And if some day we do see our children grow up to be faithful to the Lord, we know that it will be by the grace of God, and we shall give Him the glory.

166 | Two Men

Permissive Parents

Children can influence their parents just as parents can influence their children. The following story about an **imaginary** couple may have been duplicated in the lives of many of our readers.

George and Mary were a wonderful couple as they began their life together. Throughout their youth they had received strong teaching concerning worldliness and their conduct showed the effects of that teaching. They had been taught faithfulness in attendance and they never missed a service for "anything." In character and conviction, they were blameless.

This young couple failed, however, to instill into the hearts of their children these same convictions. Consequently, as the children reached their teens, they began to put pressure on their parents to let them do what all the other young people were doing. Gradually the will of the parents was broken down, and they began to permit their children to do things they never dreamed **their** children would do.

Rationalization came easy for George and Mary. "After all, the Bible is not specific in these matters," they thought. "The Bible says 'modest apparel,' but it doesn't define modesty." "And, they're only planning to **go** to the dance; they aren't planning to dance." "We can't say 'no' to everything," they said. When Junior began to show unusual athletic ability, the question of attending services became a problem. At first they took Junior out of games and brought him to midweek services, but then the team began to depend more and more on him. The play-offs came, and the team's only hope in the play-offs was for Junior to play. George and Mary gave in. And once they had given in, they had no more argument for the future. Junior never missed another game to "go to church."

George and Mary often found themselves on the defensive in Bible classes. They began to argue for their children's behavior. And, the more accustomed they became to their children's actions, the more innocent their actions seemed to be. Eventually, their own conduct became affected. They reached the point where they thought nothing of missing on Friday night during a meeting to see Junior play ball. Mary even adopted some of the daughter's dress habits, although remaining sufficiently "discreet" to stay in the good graces of the brethren. Yes, George and Mary are still in good standing in the church, and their change has been so gradual that many fail to realize that they are not the strong Christians they formerly were. What happened to George and Mary? Instead of bringing their children "up" in the nurture and admonition of the "Lord," their children brought them "down" in the nurture and admonition of the "devil."

Our children may do wrong, but they must not do wrong **with our permission**! We do not seek anger, but repentance. Parents, would **your** names fit in the place of "George" and "Mary" in the above story?

Jesus is Unique

Among all who ever lived upon the earth, Jesus is unique. He **was** what no other man ever was. He was "Immanuel," God with us. He **did** for mankind what no other man ever did. He died for our sins. He **deserves** what no other man ever deserved. He deserves our worship, adoration, and complete obedience. Christianity seeks to exalt Christ. He must become the heart and center of our lives.

Exalting Christ

How do we exalt Christ? We exalt Christ when we preach **His** word, when we follow **His** teaching, when we do only that which **He** authorizes, when we wear only **His** name, when we make **Him** the center of our affection and adoration, when we recognize **Him** as our only Head, Lord, and King. To do otherwise is to fail to exalt Him.

Positively No Visiting!

Recently, while visiting patients in a hospital, we observed several signs saying, "No Visiting." Then we came to a sign that said, "Positively No Visiting." I suppose some day we will find one that will read, "Absolutely Positively No Visiting." If only we could learn to respect authority so that "No Visiting" would just mean no visiting.

The attitude of many toward the Lord's authority is the same as it is toward a "No Visiting" sign. They somehow feel that they are an exception to the rule or that somehow the Lord will overlook this one instance of flouting His authority. But the same God who would not overlook Nadab and Abihu's strange fire (Lev 10.1-2), David's new cart (2 Sam 6.1-7), or Ananias and Sapphira's cover-up tactics, will not overlook our disregard for His authority.

The words "positively" and "absolutely" are not found in the King James Version of the Bible. But they are inferred in every statement and command found in the scriptures. One cannot hope to go to heaven while disregarding Christ's authority.

True Life

The goal of the gospel is to prepare people for heaven. Its emphasis centers upon happiness in a life to come rather than upon this life. "For what profit is it to a man," Jesus once asked, "if he gains the whole world, and loses his own soul?" The Lord would teach us to look through faith beyond the suffering and heartaches of this life to a life free of suffering and heartaches, to lay up treasures in heaven rather than upon the earth. He wants us in our preaching to proclaim a message of salvation through His blood, to bring to people's consideration those things that are eternal. But when we succeed in leading men and women to surrender their lives in favor of the life to come, we lead them into gaining, not only heaven, but also the peace and contentment that make for real happiness upon this earth. "He who finds his life shall lose it," Jesus said, "and he who loses his life for my sake shall find it."

Men of Conviction

A great need in the church is for men of conviction—men who know what they believe, why they believe it, and are living according to their convictions. So often we see people plunging headlong into some religious project in their eagerness to be **doing** something, when they need to be searching the scriptures to learn what God **wants** them to do. Theirs is action without conviction; zeal without knowledge. Jesus said, "Not everyone who says to Me, 'Lord, Lord,' shall enter the kingdom of heaven, but he who does the will of My Father in heaven" (Matt 7.21). In the judgment, the question will not be, "Were you religious?" but, "Did you do the Father's will?"

Moral Standards

God's moral standards are absolute and unchanging. Whatever was immoral when the scriptures were written is immoral today. Modern philosophies that would seek to justify homosexuality, premarital relations, divorce and remarriage for any cause, etc., are contrary to the Bible and are degrading to our society. The popular situation ethics concept, when left to each individual's application, easily becomes a concept of no ethics at all. This too is contrary to scripture. "And do not be conformed to this world, but be transformed by the renewing of your mind" (Rom 12.2). Christians must somehow rise above the standards of the world to live according to God's standards. Righteousness, without self-righteousness, is our goal.

Popularity

Jesus once said, "Woe to you when all men speak well of you" (Luke 6.26). A man who does the Lord's will, will not be popular with everybody. But woe is that man about whom no one speaks well, for, "A good name is to be chosen rather than great riches" (Prov 22.1). We must not **seek** for popularity; we must not **seek** for persecution. We must seek to do the Lord's will faithfully and to love our fellowman. When we do this, some will hate us, but others will appreciate us, and, seeing the reflection of Christ in our lives, will glorify God (Matt 5.16).

The Head of the Church

The church that recognizes Jesus Christ as its head does not do what the majority of its members want to do, nor does it follow the dictates of some church conference or association or synod. The church that recognizes Jesus as its head does what He has authorized in His word. Our Lord will not accept mere lip service. He said, "But why do you call Me 'Lord, Lord,' and not do the things which I say?" (Luke 6.46). Again He said, "If you love Me, keep My commandments" (John 14.15). Christ, as head of the church, has given instructions concerning its worship, its name, its organization, and its mission. It is only when we have diligently searched out those instructions and followed them that we have a right to refer to Jesus as our Head and Lord and King.

Local Church

The Lord arranged a plan by which individual Christians would pool their money (1 Cor 16.2), to be spent under a common oversight (elders—1 Pet 5.1-2), to accomplish a work to which they were all equally related. The result of this arrangement is a local church, a scriptural organization. He did **not** arrange a plan by which churches would pool their money under a common oversight (a board of directors) to accomplish a work to which they were all equally related. The result of this arrangement is a human missionary or benevolent institution, an unscriptural organization. The first is authorized by the Lord; the second is not. The first is of God; the second is of men.

Spiritual Emphasis

The church of the Lord is a spiritual body with a spiritual mission. It cannot compete with restaurants in the banqueting field, with TV in the entertainment field, or with schools in the educational field, for the Lord did not establish or equip it to function in these realms. But in teaching others concerning God's will and preparing them for heaven, the church has no peer, for it was for this purpose that the Lord built it. The church is the pillar and ground of the truth (1Tim 3.15). The church is a "spiritual house," offering up "spiritual sacrifices acceptable to God through Jesus Christ" (1 Pet 2.5). We long to see the day when churches will again recognize their God given mission and return to that spiritual emphasis taught in His word.

Church Growth

The church of the Lord experienced its greatest growth in the first century—at a time when its only organization was congregational and the local church was its largest functional unit. We fear that religious leaders of the twentieth century have organized more than they have evangelized. Funds that would have reached the evangelist in the first century are being used for society presidents, secretaries, and paperwork in the twentieth century. Big organizations can never substitute for personal zeal and dedication. The great need for today is a return to the simple organization of the churches of the New Testament and to that driving personal zeal that characterized those early disciples. When we get on fire for the Lord and go everywhere preaching the word, we will again see a great influx of souls being saved and added to the Lord's church.

Reaching the Lost

The gospel of Jesus Christ is the most precious message this world has ever known. It is a message that must be guarded and protected at all cost. The apostle Paul declared, "For I am not ashamed of the gospel of Christ, for it is the power of God to salvation for everyone who believes, for the Jew first and also for the Greek" (Rom 1.16). Those who attract people to their services by offering free trips to Six Flags or a CB rig to the lucky worshiper only cheapen the gospel and fill the churches with worldly-minded people. The gospel needs no worldly promotions; it cannot be enhanced by worldly schemes; it has no appeal to the worldly mind. But for that person who hungers and thirsts after righteousness, the gospel alone can bring satisfaction.

Selecting Prospects

God chose some lowly shepherds to be the first to hear of the birth of Christ. Jesus chose an immoral Samaritan woman to be the first person to whom He would identify Himself as the Messiah. It was to Mary Magdalene, out of whom He had cast seven devils, that He appeared first after His resurrection. God is no respecter of persons. He wants the gospel to be preached to the good and to the bad, to the rich and to the poor, to the mighty and to the lowly, to the religious and to the irreligious, to the red, yellow, black, and white. "Go into all the world and preach the gospel to every creature" (Mark 16.15).

We tend to be selective. We look for the one who in our judgment will be most receptive, for the influential person who will be a "help" to the church, for the middle-class man who will fit in socially, for the morally good who won't be a problem to us in the future. We tend to avoid alcoholics, unwed mothers, homosexuals, hippies, and dope addicts. While we might have looked on Lydia as a good prospect, we would have certainly overlooked Saul of Tarsus, or Simon the sorcerer, or the Philippian jailer. And in our selectivity, we may be overlooking our very best prospects.

The gospel shines most brightly when it turns the alcoholic to sobriety, the immoral to purity of life, the filthy to cleanliness, and the infidel to faith. "And such were some of you," Paul wrote to the Corinthians, "but you were washed, but you were sanctified, but you were justified in the name of the Lord Jesus and by the Spirit of our God" (1 Cor 6.11). Let us not underestimate the power of the gospel to change men.

Understandable Preaching

One mark of a truly good preacher is the ability to explain the difficult themes of the Bible in words that all spiritually-minded people can comprehend. Ezra serves as a great example. When he read the law of God before the people, he "gave the sense, and helped them to understand the reading" (Neh 8.8). Is anything to be gained by one's standing before an audience of people for forty minutes, if nothing that he says is understood? Are all things being done unto edification (1 Cor 14.26) when such is the case? Someone said it this way:

"Many sermons are like the peace of God; they pass all understanding." How true! How true! Let's keep it simple. The brethren will appreciate us more, and, above all, we will help them to go to heaven.

What We Give Our Children

Several years ago I visited with a lady whose sixteen-year-old daughter had suddenly disappeared. No word had been heard from her in over a week. The mother couldn't understand why her girl had run away from home. She opened a closet door. "Look at all those beautiful clothes," she said. "We wanted our daughter to be as well dressed as any other girl in school." She pointed to a TV in the corner of the room. "We had a TV in the living room, but our daughter wanted her own private TV, so we bought it for her," the mother said. Then she pointed to a typewriter. "Our daughter was taking typing, and we thought she needed a typewriter at home for practice." That couple had provided everything for their daughter except that which she needed most—**a love for God and His word**.

Parents, if you are not bringing your children to the services of the church, if you are not teaching them God's word, if you are not instilling in their hearts faith in God and submission to His will, you are failing as parents, no matter what you may be giving your children materially.

Credits

Thanks to Roger Shouse and Mike Noble for providing copies of many of the articles.

Most of the articles originally appeared in *Perspectives*, bulletin of 77th Street church of Christ, Birmingham, AL. The article entitled "The Church's Purpose" appeared in March, 1983.

These articles originally appeared in *Christianity Magazine:*

Two Men Err Regarding Grace: December, 1992

Two Men Are Members of the Same Church (original title, He Listened to the Tape): December, 1994

Two Churches Want to Grow: January, 1987

Two Men Teach God's Word (original title: Moderation in Doctrinal Stability): September, 1989

Two Parents Raise Their Children (original title: Total Domination/Total Permissiveness): June, 1995

Restoration Principles in John's Epistles: January, 1991

The Phone Call That Was Never Made: October, 1989

The Cost and Influence of Reputation: March, 1990

The Blessing of an Absolute Commitment: August, 1989

These articles originally appeared in *Guardian of Truth:*

Not Our - But His Workmanship: September 15, 1988

Not Ours - But His Might: October 6, 1988

HERITAGE
OF FAITH LIBRARY

The **DeWard Publishing Company Heritage of Faith Library** is a growing collection of classic Christian reprints. DeWard has already published or has plans to publish the following authors:

- A. B. Bruce
- Atticus G. Haygood
- H.C. Leupold
- J.W. McGarvey
- William Paley
- Albertus Pieters
- B. F. Westcott

Future authors and titles added to this series will be announced on our website.

www.deward.com

DEWARD
PUBLISHING COMPANY

More from DeWard
By Paul Earnhart

Invitation to a Spiritual Revolution
Studies in the Sermon on the Mount

Few preachers have studied the Sermon
on the Mount as intensively or spoken on
its contents so frequently and effectively as
the author of this work. His excellent and
very readable written analysis appeared first
as a series of articles in *Christianity Magazine.* By popular demand it is here offered
in one volume so that it can be more easily
preserved, circulated, read, reread and made
available to those who would not otherwise
have access to it. Foreword by Sewell Hall.
173 pages. $9.99 (PB)

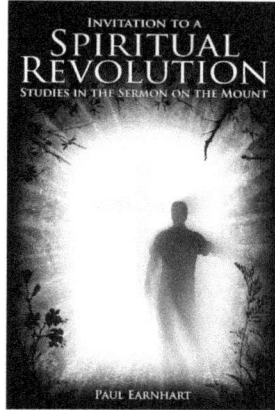

Glimpses of Eternity
Studies in the Parables of Jesus

The parables of Jesus are the compelling stories and illustrations from
our familiar world which the Lord used
to open windows for us into heaven. They
help us to understand the heart of God
and the nature of the spiritual kingdom
which His Son has brought into the world
at such an awful cost. There are messages
of comfort in the parables and some stern
warnings too. They are best understood by
those who have a longing to know God's
Son and to follow Him in genuine earnest-
ness. These studies are the compilation of
a series of articles written for *Christianity
Magazine.* 198 pages. $11.99 (PB)

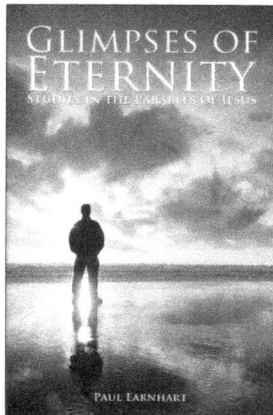

Beneath the Cross: Essays and Relfections on the Lord's Supper
Jady S. Copeland and Nathan Ward (editors)

The Bible has much to say about the Lord's Supper. Almost every component of this memorial is rich with meaning—meaning supplied by Old Testament foreshadowing and New Testament teaching. The Lord's death itself is meaningful and significant in ways we rarely point out. In sixty-nine essays by forty different authors, *Beneath the Cross* explores the depths of symbolism and meaning to be found in the last hours of the Lord's life and offers a helpful look at the memorial feast that commemorates it. 329 pages. $14.99 (PB); $23.99 (HB)

The Slave of Christ
Seth Parr

Immerse yourself in a place where sacrifice is reasonable, love and action are sensible, victory is guaranteed, and evangelism explodes. While the sacrifice of Jesus opens the door for us to Heaven, we must work to be conformed into His very image. In *The Slave of Christ,* uncover what biblical service means and how it can change your life. Energize your spiritual walk and awaken the servant within. 96 pages. $8.99 (PB)

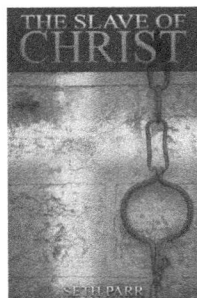

Just Jesus: The Evidence of History
James T. South

Few people are able to ignore Jesus. He has devotees and detractors, but hardly anyone is neutral about him. But how much do we know about him? Whether we love him or loathe him, it only makes sense that we know what and whom we're talking about. *Just Jesus* is about what we can know about Jesus. Jesus isn't just a religious idea but a phenomenon of history. That means we can and should ask about him all of the historical questions we can think of and see which ones can and can't be answered. Fortunately, we're able to learn a lot more about Jesus than most people think. 152 pages. $9.99 (PB)

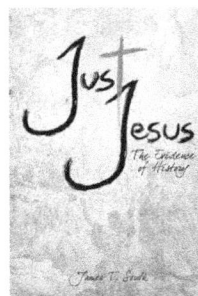

Soul Food: Lessons from Hearth to Heart
Dene Ward

Cooking has always been a part of Dene Ward's life. She grew up in a house where they were always feeding someone and followed that same path as a wife and mother. On the table, she has always offered a nourishing meal; she now offers this collection to feed your souls, lessons from her hearth to your heart. 148 pages. $9.99 (PB)

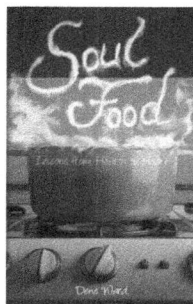

Built By the Lord: A Study of the Family
Edwin Crozier

A biblical and challenging look at the Lord-built home. *Built by the Lord* answers questions about the purpose of the Lord-built home, the roles in the Lord-built home, the goals of the Lord-built home, the habits a Lord-built home maintains, and how the Lord-built home interacts with the Lord's family. Each chapter comes packed with Biblically-based teaching, challenging personal responses, points for further meditation, and prayer to seed your own prayer life inviting God to build your home. 226 pages. $13.99 (PB)

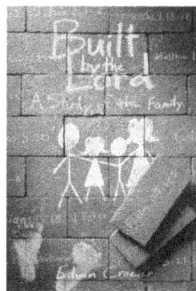

A Worthy Woman (revised edition)
Darlene Craig

Proverbs 31 presents a strong, joyful woman of wisdom, integrity, devotion, talent, industry, compassion, faith and influence. Darlene uses the example of the ideal woman to strengthen and encourage real women of all ages to further realize their "far above rubies" value as they joyfully strive to positively impact the lives of their families and others. 194 pages. $11.99 (PB)

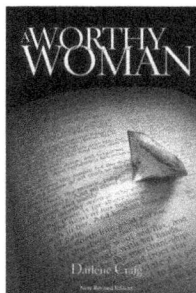

For a full listing of DeWard Publishing Company books, visit our website:

www.deward.com

www.ingramcontent.com/pod-product-compliance
Lightning Source LLC
Chambersburg PA
CBHW051825040426
42447CB00006B/379